THE NEW MERMAIDS

The Devil's Law-Case

THE NEW MERMAIDS

The Devil's Law-Case

JOHN WEBSTER

Edited by
ELIZABETH M. BRENNAN
Lecturer in English
Westfield College, University of London

ERNEST BENN LIMITED
LONDON & TONBRIDGE

First published in this form in 1975
by Ernest Benn Limited
25 New Street Square · Fleet Street · London EC4A 3JA and
Sovereign Way · Tonbridge · Kent · TN9 1RW
© Ernest Benn Limited 1975
Distributed in Canada by
The General Publishing Company Limited · Toronto
Printed in Great Britain

ISBN 0 510-34296-5 (*Paperback*)

CONTENTS

ACKNOWLEDGEMENTS

IN THE PREPARATION of this edition of *The Devil's Law-Case* I am indebted to those previous editors whose names are listed on p. xxvii. In particular I should like to acknowledge debts that I owe to F. L. Lucas's and D. C. Gunby's editions of the play; to Professor J. R. Brown's bibliographical study of it; and to R. W. Dent's book on John Webster's borrowing which contains matter of much importance besides.

I am thankful to Professor Brian Morris for guidance, sympathetic criticism, and much patience with one who was a long time finishing her work. Roma Gill read the typescript and gave invaluable advice for which I am particularly grateful.

The impetus to study *The Devil's Law-Case* was provided for me when, as a postgraduate student of The Shakespeare Institute, I participated in a reading of it directed by Professor J. R. Brown. It is a pleasure both to recall that occasion and to record my gratitude for its continued stimulation of my interest in the play over many years.

Westfield College,
University of London
May 1974

ELIZABETH M. BRENNAN

INTRODUCTION

THE AUTHOR

VERY LITTLE IS KNOWN about John Webster. He was born free (i.e.,
he had an inherited right to membership) of the Merchant Taylors'
Company but, though he was thereby entitled to attend the Merchant Taylors' School, there is no evidence of his having done so.[1]
The frequency of trial scenes and legal allusions in his plays has
given credence to the identification of the dramatist with the John
Webster who was admitted to the Middle Temple on 1 August 1598,
yet we have no external evidence of his having been a scholar. Nevertheless, the width of his reading in both classical and modern authors
and his method of dramatic composition both reveal a scholarly
mind.[2] His address to the reader of *The White Devil* expresses
admiration for the scholarly dramatists George Chapman and Ben
Jonson as well as for Beaumont and Fletcher, Shakespeare, Dekker,
and Heywood.[3]

The earliest records of John Webster's employment as a dramatist
are found in the diary of the theatre manager and financier Philip
Henslowe. Among the payments which Henslowe noted in his diary
in 1602 were those made to Webster, Munday, Middleton, Dekker,
Chettle, Thomas Heywood, and Wentworth Smith for their work
on the plays *Cæsar's Fall*, *Lady Jane*, and *Christmas Comes but Once
a Year*. It is thought that *The Famous History of Sir Thomas Wyatt*,
published in 1607, is a memorial reconstruction of the second part of
Lady Jane. The two other plays, like so many mentioned in Henslowe's diary, including Webster's *Guise*, have been lost.

In 1604 Webster wrote the Induction for John Marston's tragicomedy *The Malcontent*. He collaborated with Thomas Dekker on
two citizen comedies, *Westward Ho!* and *Northward Ho!*, which were
performed in 1604 and 1605 respectively. Webster's first tragedy,
The White Devil, was performed and published in 1612. In his
address to the reader Webster referred to the play's unsympathetic

---

[1] See R. G. Howarth, 'Two Notes on John Webster', *MLR*, LXIII (1968),
785–9.
[2] See R. W. Dent, *John Webster's Borrowing* (Berkeley and Los Angeles,
1960).
[3] See Elizabeth M. Brennan, ' "An Understanding Auditory": An Audience
for John Webster', in Brian Morris, ed., *Mermaid Critical Commentaries:
John Webster* (1970), pp. 3–19.

reception in the theatre and his own slowness in composition. Despite these conditions, he seems to have lost no time in writing *The Duchess of Malfi*, some of the material for which was derived from sources first published in 1612. The earliest date for its performance is late 1612; the latest is December 1614, the date of the death of William Ostler, the actor who created the part of Antonio Bologna.

A Monumental Column, Webster's elegy on the death of Prince Henry, the heir to the throne, was published in 1613. The sixth edition of Sir Thomas Overbury's *Characters* (1615) contained thirty-two new 'characters', including those of 'An Excellent Actor', 'A Reverent Judge', and 'An ordinarie Widdow', which were probably contributed by Webster.[4]

In his dedication of *The Devil's Law-Case* to Sir Thomas Finch three other plays by Webster which Sir Thomas has seen are named: *The White Devil*, *The Duchess of Malfi*, and *Guise*. It is, therefore, obvious that *Guise* antedated *The Devil's Law-Case* but of the play's genre we are less certain. It has usually been taken to have been a tragedy, but it may have been a comedy.[5] *The Devil's Law-Case* contains evidence of indebtedness to Ben Jonson's *The Devil is an Ass*, performed in 1616, and the *Certaine Precepts* of William Cecil, Lord Burghley, published in 1617, from which R. W. Dent has concluded that some such date as 1617 is 'surely right' for the play.[6] Internal evidence which may be seen to support a date no later than 1619 is found in at least three places. The notorious quarrels of the Chief Justice, Sir Edward Coke, and his wife which were brought to a head in 1617 may give point both to the play's subtitle – *When Women go to Law, the Devil is full of Business* – and to the exclamation of IV. i, 29-30:

> Oh women, as the ballad lives to tell you,
> What will you shortly come to?

Romelio's confident preparations in the face of death at the beginning of V. iv may reflect the bravery of Sir Walter Raleigh before his execution in November 1618.[7] One might interpret IV. ii, 570-1 as a compliment to Queen Anne.[8]

In September 1624 *The Late Murder of the Son upon the Mother, or Keep the Widow Waking* was rapidly written by Dekker, Rowley,

---

[4] See Dent, op. cit., p. 59.
[5] See R. G. Howarth, 'Webster's "Guise" ', *N&Q*, NS XIII (1966), 294-6.
[6] op.ci t., pp. 58-9. G. E. Bentley, *The Jacobean and Caroline Stage*, V (Oxford, 1958), 1250-1, urges 1610 as the date of the play.
[7] See Lucas, II, 213-16; 346-7; IV, 139; Fernand Lagarde, *John Webster* (Toulouse, 1968), pp. 474-6.
[8] See below, p. 114.

Ford, and Webster. Though it was acted often, no text survives and we only know of it through the Proceedings of the Court of Star Chamber.[9] The dates of Webster's other extant works are uncertain. Probably between 1624 and 1625 he collaborated with William Rowley and possibly Thomas Heywood on the comedy *A Cure for a Cuckold*. The minor tragedy *Appius and Virginia*, of which Webster wrote some part, though its extent is uncertain, may also belong to this period.

H. Dugdale Sykes detected Webster's collaborating hand in Middleton's comedy *Anything for a Quiet Life* (*c.* 1620–21) and Fletcher's *Fair Maid of the Inn*, first published in 1647. Accepting Sykes's arguments, F. L. Lucas included both plays in his edition of Webster's complete works. Though Webster may have contributed to *Anything for a Quiet Life*, the suggestion that he had a hand in *The Fair Maid of the Inn* has not been generally accepted.

John Webster appears to have written no other plays, though he had a share in *Arches of Triumph*, a Coronation entertainment of 1604, composed a Lord Mayor's Pageant, *Monuments of Honour*, in 1624, and was the author of some occasional verses. He died probably in the 1630s.

THE PLAY

Early Performances of Webster's Plays

Cæsar's Fall and *Lady Jane* were written for the Admiral's Men and the Earl of Worcester's Men respectively. *Westward Ho!* and *Northward Ho!* were written by Dekker and Webster for the company of Paul's Boys who presented them in their private theatre. Upon the accession of James I, the Earl of Worcester's Men changed their name to Queen Anne's Servants, or the Queen's Men, and, under their new name, they presented *The White Devil*, *The Devil's Law-Case*, and *Keep the Widow Waking* at the Red Bull, their theatre in Clerkenwell.

Webster's address to the reader of *The White Devil* relates that it was first staged in 'so dull a time of winter', in 'so open and black a theatre' that the audience was both small and unappreciative. The reference to the time of year, taken in conjunction with other evidence, enables us to date the first performance sometime in the early months of 1612.[10] It would indeed have needed a sturdy as well as enthusiastic

[9] See C. J. Sisson, *Lost Plays of Shakespeare's Age* (Cambridge, 1936), pp. 80–124.
[10] See J. R. Brown, 'On the Dating of *The White Devil* and *The Duchess of Malfi*', *PQ*, XXXI (1952), 353–62.

audience to go to a public theatre whose auditorium was open to the wintry sky to see a play which, in its intellectual content and attitude to life, was remarkably different from other plays in the repertory of the Queen's Men at that time.[11] Nearly twenty years later the title-page of the second quarto (1631) could refer to *The White Devil* as 'diuers times Acted by the Queenes Maiesties seruants' and the play had an active life in print and on stage in the Restoration.

The Duchess of Malfi was acted by the King's Men, the company which had performed *The Malcontent*, and was presented both in their private theatre in Blackfriars and in their public theatre, the Globe, between 1612 and 1614. It was revived at least once before publication in 1623. During the winter of 1630-31 it was presented both at the Cockpit theatre and at court. After the Restoration it became one of the best stock tragedies of the Duke's Company and in the early eighteenth century it was presented in the Queen's Theatre, in the Haymarket, as *The Unfortunate Duchess of Malfi or The Unnatural Brothers*.

Of the stage history of *The Devil's Law-Case* there is no evidence beyond the statement of the title-page that it was 'approouedly well Acted by her Maiesties Seruants' and the unsubstantiated comment of David Erskine Baker in *Biographia Dramatica, or a Companion to the Playhouse*, 2 vols. (1764), that it was 'a good Play, and met with Success'.[12] Though there was no seventeenth-century reprint of the play, it was not unknown. Abraham Wright noted in his Commonplace Book, *c.* 1650, that it was but an indifferent play, and continued: 'The plot is intricate enough, but if rightly scanned will be found faulty by reason many passages do either not hang together, or if they do it is so sillily that no man can perceive them likely to be ever done'.[13] The play is listed under Webster's name in Edward Phillips, *Theatrum Poetarum* (1675) and William Winstanley, *The Lives of the Most Famous English Poets* (1687).

Anything for a Quiet Life was staged by the King's Men at the Blackfriars theatre in 1621.

The Sources of the Play

Unlike his two great tragedies, Webster's tragicomedy of *The Devil's Law-Case* is not founded on the story of a famous person or family. F. L. Lucas comments simply: 'There is no source known for the plot as a whole; and it is perhaps Webster's own invention'.[14] Nevertheless, several analogues provide factual substantiation of the

[11] ibid., 355.   [12] Vol. I, Sig. F₃ʳ.
[13] Quoted in G. K. and S. K. Hunter, edd., *Penguin Critical Anthologies: John Webster* (Harmondsworth, 1969), p. 36.
[14] Lucas, II, 217.

two central and most striking scenes of the play, those of Leonora's devilish lawsuit and Contarino's cure. The tale of a mother falsely disowning her own son only to be convicted of her falsehood by a wise judge was recounted by Laurentius Venetus, *alias* Justinianus Venetus *alias* Bernardo Giustiniani, in *De Origine Urbis Gestique Venetorum* (1492) and repeated by Joannes Magnus, bishop of Uppsala, *De omnibus Gothorum Sueonumque Regibus* (Rome, 1554) and amplified by Nicholas Caussin, *La Cour sainte* (Paris, 1624). Caussin cites an additional source in a manuscript of his friend Père Sirmond.[15] A dramatic parallel is found in *Lust's Dominion or The Lascivious Queen*, a play first published in 1657 and attributed, on its title-page, to Christopher Marlowe, but which clearly belongs to the revenge tragedies of the late 1590s. It may be fairly certainly identified with *The Spanish Moor's Tragedy*, for which Henslowe made payments to John Day and Thomas Dekker in February 1600.[16] The lascivious queen of the subtitle is the Queen-Mother of Spain whose lover is the Moor Eleazar. Eleazar is anxious to avenge wrongs done to his father by destroying a number of enemies, including the Queen's son, King Philip. To further his plans the Queen agrees to arrange for the publication by two friars of the false story of her son's illegitimacy. Eleazar sees this scheme as a means of attacking both the young king and the Cardinal Mendoza who had decreed Eleazar's banishment. Thus the Moor exults:

> By this means shall you thrust him from all hopes
> Of wearing Castiles diadem, and that spur
> Galling his sides, he will flye out, and fling,
> And grind the Cardinals heart to a new edg
> Of discontent, from discontent grows treason,
> And on the stalk of treason death: he's dead
> By this blow, and by you; yet no blood shed.[17]

It may also be noted that *Lust's Dominion* has been described as the first revenge tragedy in which the thoroughgoing influence of Marlowe's *The Jew of Malta* is clearly discernible,[18] while the influence of Barabas has been remarked in the characterization of Romelio in *The Devil's Law-Case*.[19]

Perhaps a closer parallel to Leonora's situation may be found in

[15] ibid., 219–21.
[16] See Alfred Harbage, *Annals of English Drama*, revised by S. Schoenbaum (1964), pp. 76–8.
[17] *Materials for the Study of the Old English Drama, New Series, 5: Lust's Dominion*, ed., J. Le Gay Brereton (Louvain, 1931), lines 907–15.
[18] Fredson Bowers, *Elizabethan Revenge Tragedy, 1587–1642* (Princeton, 1940), pp. 272–3.
[19] See Lucas, II, 217–18.

William Warner's *Continuance of Albion's England* (1606), XVI, cv: 'Of *Nest*, Lady of Brechnock, her dishonourable Reuenge against her owne Sonne', a source identified by R. W. Dent.[20] Nest, like the Queen-Mother of *Lust's Dominion*, becomes lascivious after her husband's death. Her son Mahel fights her lover and, to avenge this audacity, she resolves to transfer his birthright to his sister. Accordingly, 'winged thus by *Nemesis*' she hastens to reveal to King Henry II the false story of her own dishonour:

> *Mahel* my Sonne (ah, would he were not scandalously such,
> But for he is, it is it that so deeply doth me touch)
> I bore in Bastardie, and for I therein did amis,
> I hold me iustly plagued that my Plague a Bastard is.
> I have a vertuous Daughter by my valerous Husband, She
> Inherit should his State: Vouchsafe, my Leage, it so may be.

Nest swears her false oath; her son is disinherited. Nest dies, and her daughter Sibyl, enriched with her brother's lands, married Miles, Earl of Hereford. William Camden, the classical scholar and historian who taught Ben Jonson at Westminster School, gave an abbreviated version of this story in his *Britannia . . . Chorographica descriptio*, a work first published in Latin in 1586, enlarged in later editions, and translated into English in 1610 by Philemon Holland.

The happy accident of a man's life being saved by the stab of a would-be assassin was well known in antiquity and to the Elizabethans. The story, usually related of the tyrant Jason of Pherae, told how the dagger meant to kill him pierced an abscess and thus saved his life. It is recounted or mentioned by such classical authors as Pliny, Cicero, Seneca, and Plutarch. Webster's immediate source was probably Simon Goulart's *Histoires Admirables* (Paris, 1600), translated by Edward Grimeston as *Admirable and Memorable Histories* in 1607, and from which Webster borrowed twice in writing the last act of *The Duchess of Malfi*. Goulart's story is, appropriately, of a vengeful Italian who, having sought out his enemy, said to be at the point of death, entered his sick-room, gave him certain stabs with his dagger, and fled. In Grimeston's translation the narration concludes: 'They binde vp this poore sicke mans wounds, who by the meanes of so great a losse of blood, recouered his health. So hee recouered his health and life, by his meanes who sought his death'.[21]

Webster's Tragicomedy of *The Devil's Law-Case*

For the Elizabethans and Jacobeans the great certainties of life were seen to be revealed in God's relationships with man, recorded in

[20] op. cit., pp. 308-9.
[21] See Lucas, II, 217; Dent, op. cit., 246-7, 249, 304-5.

Biblical history or illustrated by contemporary events.[22] Whether or not he accepted the Calvinistic doctrine of predestination, Renaissance man recognized very clearly – as his medieval ancestors had done – the conditions under which he might merit salvation or damnation. The secularization of drama, markedly accelerated in the Jacobean age, may be seen to be characterized by a preoccupation with the great uncertainties of life, revealed especially in man's relationships with man. More specifically, Jacobean drama paralleled the mood of much metaphysical poetry in directing the audience's attention to the perhaps greater uncertainties of women's relationships with man, and in so doing drama and poetry made use of irony and satire, both defensive and offensive.

The dominant theme of Jacobean literature – the questioning of accepted values — did not spring suddenly into prominence. Its emergence is clearly visible in, for instance, those characters who cannot be absorbed into the happy and idealistic world of Shakespeare's middle comedies: Shylock, Jacques, and Malvolio. Nevertheless, there are sound reasons for thinking of this theme as characteristically Jacobean, since the greatest uncertainties in English life at the turn of the century were caused by the prospect and, later, the reality of the change in sovereign from an old English queen to a middle-aged Scottish king. Of the social and political chaos in London in the early days of the reign of James I an anonymous contemporary commentator reported:

> In outχrward] appearance Papists were favoured, masses almost publiquely administred, Protestants discountenanced, dishonest men honored, those that were little lesse then Sorcerers and witches preferred, private quarrels nourished, but especially betweene the Scottishe and the Englishe, duells in every streete mainteined:...[23]

The eruption of the Gunpowder Plot in November 1605 caused an immediate and violent alteration in at least the first of these conditions; but duelling continued until the king issued Proclamations against it in 1613 and 1614, and against the carrying of pistols and daggers in 1616. It is, therefore, significant that duels and discussions of duelling ethics are prominent in such Jacobean plays as Chapman's *Bussy D'Ambois*, written between 1600 and 1604, and Middleton and Rowley's *A Fair Quarrel*, belonging to 1615-17, both of which, like *The Devil's Law-Case*, are also concerned with the reliability of women.

[22] The history of the Duchess of Malfi, for instance, was included in Thomas Beard's *The Theatre of God's Judgements* (1597).
[23] *The Secret History of ye Reign of K. James ye I^{st}*: BM Harley MS 4888, o. 214^r.

The same two themes were, indeed, also present in Shakespeare's turn-of-the-century tragedy, *Hamlet*. The Prince of Denmark recognizes the demands of the code of honour:

> Rightly to be great
> Is not to stir without great argument,
> But greatly to find quarrel in a straw
> When honour's at the stake.   (IV. iv, 53–6)

He also questions the trustworthiness of his mother and of Ophelia, the girl whom he has loved. Yet, though *Hamlet* may adumbrate Jacobean tragedy in two of its themes, the distinctive and pervasive Jacobean tone is lacking: a fact made obvious from a comparison of Hamlet's meditation on Yorick's skull in the graveyard (V. i) with Vindice's attitude to the skull of his poisoned love in *The Revenger's Tragedy*, which was acted between 1606 and 1607 (I, i and III. v).

In one important sense a son's attitude to his mother was of very particular concern to Jacobean Englishmen, since the possibility of King James exacting vengeance for the execution of his Catholic mother by the Protestant English might well depend on his attitude to her. Neither in reality nor in common repute had Mary Queen of Scots provided would-be assessors of her honesty – in all the connotations of the word – with clear and unambiguous evidence. Her character, in its combination of such apparently irreconcilable opposites as unchastity and piety, defied analysis in exactly the same way as the character of Vittoria Accoramboni, Webster's white devil: a fact of which the original audiences of Webster's tragedy were probably aware.[24]

Was Vittoria a saint . . . or a devil? The very title of the play is a paradox. Is the white devil a devil transformed into an angel; a devil in crystal? Does Vittoria corrupt others, or is she herself corrupted by others? If she is corrupted, is it by her own nature – her blood – or by her brother, who is of her blood? Is she corrupted by Brachiano; or does he corrupt her? More important, does either of them really love the other? As I have suggested elsewhere,[25] Webster himself refused to judge or classify the characters of his tragic heroines, thus challenging his audience to judge for themselves where good and evil lay. The questions about Vittoria which tease the audience of *The White Devil* are precisely those which must have teased people who knew her in life. Similarly, the character of the Duchess of Malfi defies both judgement and righteous indignation. At first sight, the character of Giovanna d'Aragona, heroine of Webster's second major tragedy, would appear to be much less ambiguous than that of

[24] See Lucas, I, 96.
[25] Brennan, op. cit.

Vittoria, whose reputation must have lent credence to the totally inaccurate description of her on the title-page of the first quarto edition of the play as 'the famous Venetian Curtizan'. But the Duchess was a young widow, and there were those who thought that for widows to remarry was a sign of lasciviousness. She was a duchess, one for whom marriage to a commoner, like her major-domo, was out of the question. She was mother, moreover, to the young Duke of Amalfi who might be scandalized by her behaviour. She was also sister to two powerful men, the Cardinal of Aragon and the Marquis of Gerace (Webster's Ferdinand). Powerful in the church, her brother Cardinal was also a soldier. In an age when few women of her rank would have been allowed freedom of choice in marriage, the only way in which the young Duchess could marry Antonio Bologna was in secret. In order to marry in secret she had to deceive her brothers and, incidentally, the common people of the dukedom of Amalfi, who believed her to be a strumpet.

What has been observed here of Vittoria and the Duchess of Malfi may also be applied to Leonora and Jolenta, the almost tragic heroines of *The Devil's Law-Case*. As a son and a brother Romelio doubts their trustworthiness. Between brother and mother Jolenta is forced into a marriage contract against her will. Deception, disguise, and escape are her only means of avoiding some of its consequences. Self-deceived, Leonora turns in vengeance on her son, practising more deceit to try to have him disinherited. Like the two tragedies, *The Devil's Law-Case* forces us to consider whether deceit – especially in a woman – can ever be justified.

In one sense the world of Webster's major plays was both secular and contemporary; the atmosphere which it shared with the rest of Jacobean drama was startlingly realistic in its cynicism. Yet, no matter how secular, contemporary, or realistic the atmosphere and characters of their plays, the major Jacobean dramatists relied on their audience's familiarity with orthodox Christian values to provide a framework of reference, a basis of normality, for their work. For all its Jacobean tone, *The Revenger's Tragedy* depends for its moral point on its audience's knowledge of the medieval concept of the Seven Deadly Sins. One of the play's most memorable lines – 'When the bad bleeds, then is the tragedy good' – confounds the precepts of Aristotle to pronounce a moral justification for a form of art so greatly concerned with misery and bloodshed. In this connection it should be noted that, though the genre of revenge tragedy was dominant on the English stage from the first production of *The Spanish Tragedy*, probably in the late 1580s, until the closing of the theatres in 1642, the change from Elizabethan to Jacobean is discernible in a marked shift in theme from revenge for murder to

revenge for honour. Though honour as a concept was capable of an
extremely wide range of interpretation,[26] the Jacobean dramatists
were particularly concerned with female honour: the honour in-
herent in a woman's chastity which, if lost, would bring ruin to all
her menfolk as well as herself. As death was preferable to dishonour,
the question of whether or not a woman was really honest was an
extremely vital one for the Jacobean gentleman. *Othello*, though the
most Jacobean of Shakespeare's major tragedies, is, nevertheless,
like the other three, primarily concerned with the tragic hero. Jacobean tragedies of honour by Middleton and Ford, no less than
Webster's major tragedies, Heywood's *A Woman Killed with Kindness*, and Beaumont and Fletcher's *The Maid's Tragedy*, are dominated
by their tragic heroines.

One of John Webster's most original contributions to English
tragedy consisted in his examination of the characteristics which
combine to produce a convincing tragic heroine. We might say that,
in Desdemona, Shakespeare had already done this: but Shakespeare's
tragedy is virtually presented from a masculine point of view. It is,
however, true that Desdemona's innocence is tempered with sufficient wilfulness to make adverse attitudes to her credible. She contracted a secret marriage which, to many observers, must have seemed
to go against nature.

> Look to her, Moor, if thou hast eyes to see:
> She has deceiv'd her father, and may thee. (I. iii, 292–3)

Brabantio's taunt, later echoed by Iago, festers in Othello's mind,
while Roderigo is easily persuaded that Desdemona will prostitute
herself to him for cash. Similarly, the characterization of Ophelia
is compounded of elements which make the questions of her loyalty –
to her father and to Hamlet – and her innocence open to debate.[27]

While providing a convincing answer to the question, 'What did
this woman do to merit death?', the tragedy which successfully presents a sympathetic tragic heroine must also be concerned with the
question, 'Can this woman be trusted?' It is not a matter of one
woman being able to trust another – that was left for a later dramatist,
Thomas Middleton, to explore in *Women Beware Women* (*c.* 1620–27)
– but it is a matter of whether one man or many men can trust one
particular woman. In Webster's major tragedies this point is
emphasized by the strange situation of his heroines. Both Vittoria
and the Duchess of Malfi move in exclusively masculine worlds;

[26] See C. L. Barber, *The Idea of Honour in the English Drama, 1591–1700*
(Gothenburg, 1957).
[27] See Harold Jenkins, 'Hamlet and Ophelia', *Proceedings of the British
Academy*, XLIX (1963), 131–51.

both appear to be cut off from contact with other women; both are virtually isolated from the friendship or companionship of women of their own rank. Their waiting-women are their only companions. Vittoria's mother, Cornelia, appears beside her, in sane wrath and, later, in distracted grief; but there is no impression given of any close relationship between mother and daughter. We may also note that Desdemona was similarly isolated.

It has been necessary to say thus much of Jacobean tragedy because the genre to which *The Devil's Law-Case* belongs, tragi-comedy, far from being evenly poised between the extremes of tragedy and comedy, was usually quite heavily weighted towards tragedy, and relied for many of its effects on the themes, atmos-phere, and characterization of that form. So *The Devil's Law-Case* embodies the potentially tragic theme of the untrustworthiness of women and to this Webster adds a parallel theme, of equal tragic potential, of the untrustworthiness of men. If Romelio is in danger of being ruined by his mother, his sister, Jolenta, is in danger of being ruined by him. Contrary to what one would expect of an honourable man, he is quite careless of his sister's reputation,[28] and would use her misfortune to make her appear the mother of his own expected bastard by the nun Angiolella. But Romelio is not a gentleman. 'The Fortunate Young Man' – as he is called – is an exceedingly hard businessman. The atmosphere of the play is harsh and mercantile, for its world is that of commerce and law. Thus Leonora and Jolenta, no less than Vittoria and the Duchess of Malfi, are threatened by the values of a male-dominated society. When Leonora turns against her, Jolenta finds companionship in misery in the debauched nun Angiolella. Leonora herself, like Vittoria and the Duchess of Malfi, admits only her waiting-woman, Winifred, to her confidence.

In the characterization of Leonora as a selfish, vain, foolish, and middle-aged woman we see something of Webster's power of feminine character portrayal which distinguished his great tragedies. It is because Leonora is presented as a vacillating, even a pathetic woman, that Webster is able to endow her speeches with both flashes of feminine spite and flashes of great beauty. Thus, when she learns that Romelio has killed Contarino, the young suitor to her daughter with whom she herself has fallen in love, Leonora's exclamations of frustration contain a simple and moving confession:

> For as we love our youngest children best,
> So the last fruit of our affection,
> Wherever we bestow it, is most strong,

[28] See Elizabeth M. Brennan, 'The Relationship between Brother and Sister in the Plays of John Webster', *MLR*, LVIII (1963), 488–94 (489).

> Most violent, most unresistible,
> Since 'tis indeed our latest harvest-home,
> Last merriment 'fore winter; and we widows,
> As men report of our best picture-makers,
> We love the piece we are in hand with better
> Than all the excellent work we have done before.
> And my son has deprived me of all this. . . .
>
> (III. iii, 246–55)

Like Shakespeare in *The Winter's Tale*, Webster here reminds us how bitterly love and the pangs of jealousy may be experienced by the middle-aged.

The subtitle of the play is *When Women go to Law, the Devil is full of Business*, but it is not until the latter part of Act III, Scene iii that Leonora conceives the idea of the devilish lawsuit which will constitute her revenge on Romelio for the deprivation of which she has been heard to speak so forcefully. Earlier in the play, and again, later, it is her young daughter Jolenta who commands our interest.

The play opens with a discussion between two merchants, Prospero and Romelio, from which we learn, first, that Romelio is enormously wealthy and, secondly, that he is avaricious. Seeing the approach of the great lord Contarino, Prospero says that he knows, of course, what Contarino's business in Leonora's – that is, Romelio's – house is. Romelio, too, is quite aware of Contarino's interest in Jolenta, but he is anxious to break this proposed alliance, if he can. He despises Contarino's suit because, though nobly born, Contarino is poor. Romelio alleges:

> . . . he makes his colour
> Of visiting us so often, to sell land,
> And thinks if he can gain my sister's love,
> To recover the treble value.   (I. i, 37–40)

Prospero protests –

>   Sure he loves her
> Entirely, and she deserves it.   (I. i, 40–1)

But Romelio insists:

>   Faith, though she were
> Crook'd-shouldered, having such a portion,
> She would have noble suitors: but truth is,
> I would wish my noble venturer take heed,
> It may be whiles he hopes to catch a gilthead
> He may draw up a gudgeon.   (I. i. 41–6)

Webster thus makes Romelio's attitude to Jolenta quite clear. But what of the attitude of her suitor Contarino? This is left ambiguous. Contarino is unaware of the extent of Romelio's knowledge of his interest in Jolenta. He begs Romelio's pardon for having engaged himself thus far in a business – and the word is significant – in which Romelio should have been considered. Contarino does not want the world to know

> what wealthy voyage
> I went about, till I had got the mine
> In mine own possession.   (I. i, 79–81)

Whether Contarino considers Jolenta or her wealth the greater treasure remains uncertain. Contarino later reveals himself to be either so careful or so cunning in his speech – or both – that Leonora believes that she, and not Jolenta, is beloved by him. The conclusion of the play, in which Leonora is apparently paired off with Contarino, and Jolenta with the same Ercole to whom she had been contracted against her will, has offended some critics. The lack of stage directions, as Lucas has noted,[29] makes the denouement ambiguous for the reader, though it must be clarified for an audience. One might remark that exactly the same kind of ambiguity is present at the conclusion of *Measure for Measure*, and that in both plays the precise action resolved on in production should clarify the moral issues of the play. In *The Devil's Law-Case* the ambiguous presentation of Contarino, together with the quite unambiguous fact of his being a reckless and unsuccessful gambler, suggests not only that he is untrustworthy, but that he is quite the wrong husband for Jolenta. At least Leonora has the cash as well as the desire to indulge his expensive tastes. It is, surely, as fitting that she should be paired off with Contarino as it is that the noble Ercole should have won the fair Jolenta by his exceptionally honourable behaviour.

For the Jacobeans the pattern of tragicomedy was outlined by one of its greatest practitioners, John Fletcher, in a definition borrowed from Giovanni Battista Guarini (1538–1612), author of *Il Pastor Fido*:

> A tragie-comedie is not so called in respect of mirth and killing but in respect it wants deat[h]s, which is inough to make it no tragedie, yet brings some neere it, which is inough to make it no comedie: which must be a representation of familiar people, with such kinde of trouble as no life be questiond, so that a God is as lawfull in this as in a tragedie, and meane people as in a comedie.[30]

In practice Fletcherian tragicomedy was quite distinctive;[31] yet in

[29] Lucas, II, 362–3.
[30] John Fletcher, *The Faithfvll Shepheardesse* (n.d.), Sig. ¶₂ᵛ.
[31] See Philip Edwards, 'The Danger Not the Death', *Stratford-upon-Avon Studies I: Jacobean Theatre*, edd. J. R. Brown and B. Harris (1960), pp. 158–77.

theory this definition could be applied to *Measure for Measure*, *Much Ado About Nothing*, *Cymbeline*, and – if one excepts the off-stage deaths of Mamillius and Antigonus – to *The Winter's Tale*. It is remarkable that a number of Jacobean dramatists brought their characters near to death, or allowed them to think that they had been responsible for someone else's death, in order that they might learn something of the importance of life.[32] If we recognize that this aim is achieved in *The Devil's Law-Case* no less for the audience than for the victims and survivors on stage, we may see how the writing of this play demonstrated neither deflection of purpose nor diminution of artistic talent on Webster's part. I would agree with D. C. Gunby:

> Basic to my view of Webster is a belief that he was essentially a didacticist (albeit a didacticist of genius), and that his career shows a steady progression from implicit to explicit methods of conveying his message. In *The Devil's Law-Case* that progression reaches its logical conclusion in a thesis play.[33]

As a didacticist Webster relied, no less than Middleton, Massinger, and Ford, on his audience's knowledge of Christian doctrine, and in this reliance was not therefore original. He was, however, both original and unique in refraining from passing judgement on his characters and thus challenging his audience to consider problems which we today call problems of situational ethics. It is a commonplace of criticism of Jacobean drama that it abounds in striking individual scenes which may be found in plays which, *in toto*, lack coherence. This criticism has indeed been applied to both Webster's major tragedies. In *The Devil's Law-Case*, though we are struck by the force of the trial scene, in particular, we may well be more aware of situations than of scenes in the play as a whole. For the situations – or predicaments – in which the characters find themselves are extreme, and extremely varied. They may also be seen to be extremely comic. The tension of the trial scene is comic tension. And yet, though we know that the Don Crispiano, who, with the aid of tennis-court woollen slippers and julep, was said to have fathered Romelio, is the very judge hearing Leonora's suit; though we know that Winifred is only pretending to be an old bawd; though her attempts to prove her great age provide us with real farce, as does Sanitonella's production of his 'very lovely' meat pie from his buckram bag, the imagery of the play reminds us, as D. C. Gunby has shown, of the 'insidiously corrupting effect that law-suits such as Leonora's have

---

[32] I have amplified this point in ' "An Understanding Auditory": An Audience for John Webster', pp. 9–11.

[33] D. C. Gunby, '*The Devil's Law-Case*: An Interpretation', *MLR*, LXIII (1968), 546.

on society'.[34] Angiolella, the pregnant nun – even such a factual description of her state provokes unholy amusement – is in an extreme situation when she meets Jolenta who is running away in disguise, as a moor. The stage direction tells us that Angiolella is 'great-bellied', but the discussion of Jolenta's feigned pregnancy surely heightens our awareness of the padding which produces theatrical pregnancy. Similarly, Romelio's self-confessed Machiavellian villainy in the disguise of an Italianated Jew possesses a theatrical quality which must make our attitude toward him, to say the least, ambivalent. And what are we to make of the other contrasting extremes of Romelio's character, his poetic impulses and utterances – whether serious or mock-serious, like his dirge – and his bravery in the face of death? Where *The White Devil* and *The Duchess of Malfi*, especially in their fifth acts, present problems which are difficult for actors to overcome, *The Devil's Law-Case* contains ambiguities of characterization and tone which only stage performance can resolve.

One aspect of *The Devil's Law-Case* which both distinguishes it from and links it to Webster's major tragedies is his interpretation of the great uncertainties of life as originating, not simply in man's or woman's relationships with man, but in the devil's relationships with man. The opposition of the great certainties of life seen in God's relationships with man and the great uncertainties seen in the devil's relationships with man is both simple and traditional. The connection between woman and the devil is as old as the story of Genesis. Though Webster's interest in the devil and his powers is perhaps more obvious in *The White Devil* than in *The Duchess of Malfi*, it is declared in the latter play in references to witches (e.g., I. ii, 230–2); in the suspicion that the Duchess has been bewitched (III. i, 63–7; 72–9); in the definition of an intelligencer as a 'very quaint invisible devil in flesh' (I. ii, 181); in Ferdinand's recognition of the devil in his brother Cardinal (V. v, 50–1); in Bosola's comment on the devil's work (I. ii, 196–8); and in Antonio's comment on the way the devil works on Bosola (II. i, 97–8).[35]

The Devil and the Vice were well-known figures of early English drama.[36] Both art and theology, from earliest times, had emphasized that the devil's chief characteristic, next to pride, was his ability to assume a physically pleasing shape and to project a deceptively pleasing personality. Nevertheless, men continued to expect all that

---

[34] ibid., 549.
[35] See D. C. Gunby, '*The Duchess of Malfi*: A Theological Approach', in Brian Morris, ed., *Mermaid Critical Commentaries: John Webster*, pp. 181–204.
[36] See L. W. Cushman, *The Devil and the Vice in the English Dramatic Literature before Shakespeare* (1900; 1970).

was fair to be good. Babes, as Vittoria recognized, were terrified, not by attractively evil shapes, but by painted devils. The foul fiend who converses with Launcelot Gobbo, in *The Merchant of Venice*, Act II, Scene ii, is a decidedly sympathetic character; he belongs to our world. So, too, do the characters of *The Devil's Law-Case*, and the comic aspects of corruption and deception which the play reveals bring home to us how often and how easily we may retreat from a real confrontation with the devil into embarrassed laughter and disbelief in his existence.

Webster certainly believed in the devil, and his belief is nowhere more obvious than in this play. The climax of the play's tension rests on the question of whether or not Leonora and the Capuchin will be released from their imprisonment in the turret in time to stop the duel between Romelio and Ercole. Romelio's unexpected relenting is an answer to their prayer for release. A personal devil is responsible for the evil in the world of the play; belief in a personal God produces the final resolution of difficulties, and evil is converted to good. The point is underlined by the fact that both good and evil have been seen to operate through the same person, Leonora. This is a much more didactic statement of a Christian viewpoint than Webster had allowed himself in his major tragedies. The question to be asked is: is satiric tragicomedy the right context for such a statement?

Since the stories of Vittoria and the Duchess of Malfi were based on historical truth, Webster could not 'save' either of them from death through their own or others' prayers. In both plays the highest churchmen, the Cardinals, one of whom becomes Pope, are evil men. Integrity of life is the only value which either heroine can assert in the face of evil. The Duchess of Malfi may make a good end, but neither her life nor Vittoria's had a happy ending. So the only way to present these murder stories in tragic form was to set them in a completely evil world. At least the audience is allowed, in the last act of each play, to see some kind of justice, even if it is only the 'wild justice' of revenge meted out to the murderers of the tragic heroines. Whereas in his major tragedies Webster deliberately refrained from equating his heroines' deaths with the wages of sin, in *The Devil's Law-Case* sin is seen to bring some of the central characters very near to death; repentance and prayer purge the evil and death is avoided. Given the development of Webster's art, satiric tragicomedy was the only context for this statement.

Webster's career as a dramatic poet undoubtedly reached its peak in his great tragedies. Nevertheless, his poetic qualities, expressing a shrewd observation of human nature and the truths of human experience, are just as evident in *The Devil's Law-Case*. There is a passage in the play which, both in conversational tone and the use of the rhythms of living speech, is very reminiscent of the work of T. S. Eliot.[37] Addressing her waiting-woman, Winifred, Leonora says:

> Thou hast lived with me
> These forty years; we have grown old together,
> As many ladies and their women do,
> With talking nothing, and with doing less:
> We have spent our life in that which least concerns life,
> Only in putting on our clothes; . . .   (III. iii, 372–7)

These lines may serve to illustrate one of the changes in language from that of the great tragedies: the tone is relaxed; the poetry is the poetry of everyday, domestic utterance; it lacks tragic intensity. More than that, the poetry is about everyday things, and though Leonora is capable of elevation of speech, her thought is not habitually on the elevated plane of the Duchess of Malfi, for instance. When the Duchess and Antonio joke with Cariola in the bedroom scene (III. ii) they lapse quite naturally into 'vain poetry', spiced with classical references. One would not expect this of any of the characters in *The Devil's Law-Case*. Nevertheless, the range of poetic effects and of types of poetic utterance in the play is considerable. Extremes in situation and contrasts and parallels of character and image are accordingly matched by the verse.

Imagery in *The Devil's Law-Case* performs the same functions as it does in the two great tragedies. It is a means whereby Webster presents themes which are woven into the plot, but are equally important on their own. As the world of the play is, initially, mercantile, we find the poetry loaded with images of gold, silver, jewels, and treasure. Riches and wealth are frequently mentioned; so is trade. There is talk of accounts; of contracts – not only marriage contracts; and bargains – which include marriage. The word 'business' is used to mean 'affair' and 'matter', and many topics of high import are reduced to a mere commercial level. The central scene is a trial scene, and there are many legal images and images relative to abuses of the law. Ercole's reference, in II. iv, 8–10, to false executors who swindle orphans, relates the corruption of the play to extremely ancient practices and also anticipates Romelio's plans for his own illegitimate child to inherit two fortunes. The plight of Jolenta, harassed by her brother and her mother, is stressed by images of

---

[37] Inga-Stina Ewbank, 'Webster's Realism or, "A Cunning Piece Wrought Perspective"', in Brian Morris, ed., *Mermaid Critical Commentaries: John Webster*, p. 173 says that this speech 'might almost have come out of *The Family Reunion*'. It also suggests lines from 'The Love Song of J. Alfred Prufrock', especially 'I have measured out my life with coffee spoons'.

madness and witchcraft. Such images are also applied to Leonora. As in *The White Devil* and *The Duchess of Malfi*, images serve to juxtapose arresting and contrasting ideas: beggars and begging; which is more valuable, money or life?

Among the characters, too, there are interesting contrasts. There are the two heirs, Julio, Crispiano's son, and Jolenta, heiress to Contarino and Ercole, potential heiress to her dead father's fortune. There are good and bad lawyers: those who will not and those who will take bribes to take up Leonora's lawsuit. There are two feigned penitents: Leonora in court; Romelio in his earliest encounters with the Capuchin. Later they both become real penitents.

There are also contrasts between the contexts in which similar words are spoken. Romelio's mock dirge, beginning

> All the flowers of the spring
> Meet to perfume our burying: (V. iv, 112–13)

echoes an earlier image found in his comment on the news of Contarino's death:

> Poor Jolenta! Should she hear of this,
> She would not after the report keep fresh
> So long as flowers in graves.   (II. iii, 137–9)

The commentary on life in *The Devil's Law-Case* is provided by many characters, but most consistently by Romelio. Though this suggests comparison of him with Bosola or Flamineo, he is neither a discontented scholar, an intriguer, nor a parasite. One form of counterpart to Bosola and Flamineo may be seen to be provided by Winifred. Yet the parallel cannot be closely drawn. She is as bawdy as Juliet's nurse; does what she is told, not what she is bribed to do; and the discovery of her perjury is very comic.

The fabric of this play contains fewer borrowings from other authors than the major tragedies. However, as the notes to this edition indicate, there are some interesting examples of Webster's having returned to a source of borrowing in one of the tragedies in order to rephrase it, as well as re-use it. Perhaps the most important borrowings are those made from *The White Devil* and *The Duchess of Malfi* themselves. Though many of these are pointed out in the notes, their effect depends not on the conning of footnotes, but on the reader's ability to hear a Websterian echo in his own mind. It is as if Webster himself were insisting that we see all three plays in relation to each other. *The Devil's Law-Case* is certainly a different play from the twin masterpieces, and is indeed a lesser play, but is not unworthy to stand beside them for our consideration in assessing the achievement of John Webster.

NOTE ON THE TEXT

THIS EDITION of *The Devil's Law-Case* is based on the 1623 quarto which has been collated with the editions of Dyce, Hazlitt, and Lucas, modernized throughout, and emended where necessary. The original punctuation has been altered only where its retention might prove ambiguous or confusing for a modern reader: e.g., a colon followed by a capital is reproduced as a full stop and, where appropriate, a question mark has been replaced with an exclamation mark, as very few of the latter occur in the quarto.

The verse of the play contains fewer elisions than that of *The Duchess of Malfi* or *The White Devil*. The reader or actor is never required to stress the final syllable of a word ending in – *ed* in order to make the verse scan. Therefore, in accordance with the principles of the New Mermaid series, no distinction is made in the text between words originally spelt with an – *ed* ending and those with a -*t* or -'*d* ending; *ere* (= ever) is modernized as *e'er*; *ore* as *o'er*; the variants *O* and *Oh* are regularized as *Oh*. Numerals and ampersands in the original have been expanded in this text.

The 1623 quarto contained act divisions only, and so the scene divisions established by Dyce have been introduced. Emendations of, additions to, and relocations of stage directions have been kept to the minimum and all changes from the original are indicated by the use of square brackets in the text and, where necessary, notes in the collations. The Latin phrases which indicate act divisions have been silently regularized.

The more important collations are recorded beneath the text. Minor collations, together with longer textual notes, are provided in Textual Appendix A.

The greatest difficulty facing an editor of *The Devil's Law-Case* is caused by irregularity in the line division of the quarto. Though one is tempted to blame the compositor for this, one feels, nevertheless, as a recent editor has remarked, 'that Webster is employing an irregular pattern that comes close to everyday speech'.[38] What I have said of the unaccented -*ed* word endings and of the conversational tone of the verse[39] confirms this impression. An editor's interpretation of this pattern of everyday speech is, however, bound to be very subjective, and so I have provided, in Textual Appendix B, a collation of variant readings in the editions of Dyce, Hazlitt, and Lucas which affect the verse structure, these editions being less

[38] Frances A. Shirley, ed., *John Webster, The Devil's Law-Case*, Regents Renaissance Drama Series (1972), p. xxiii.

[39] See above, pp. xxii–xxiii.

readily available for comparison than those of D. C. Gunby and Frances A. Shirley.

Though the text of the quarto provides no conclusive evidence of the nature of the printer's copy, two corrections – at IV. i, 15 and V. i, 35 – suggest that Webster may have overseen the printing.

For this edition I have used the following copies of the quarto: British Museum 644. f. 71; Bodleian Library Malone 199 (7); Victoria and Albert Museum Dyce 10493 (Dyce 26, Box 47/4). The last named is the only correct copy, of the five extant, in Britain. BM 644. f. 71 has C outer forme in the uncorrected state; Bodley Mal. 199 (7) has K outer forme in the uncorrected state. Two other British Museum copies are imperfect and unreliable, Ashley 2206 being one of T. J. Wise's forgeries, perfected by sheets stolen from BM 82. c. 26(2).

ABBREVIATIONS

IN COLLATIONS and notes the following abbreviations are used:

Q   the quarto of 1623.
Qa   the uncorrected quarto.
Qb   the corrected state of the quarto.
Dent   R. W. Dent, *John Webster's Borrowing* (Berkeley and Los Angeles, 1960).
Dyce   Alexander Dyce, *The Works of John Webster* (1857), a revision of his edition of 1830.
ed.   editor edd. editors..
Gunby   *John Webster: Three Plays*, edited by D. C. Gunby (Harmondsworth, 1972).
Hazlitt   W. C. Hazlitt, *The Dramatic Works of John Webster* (1857), Vol. III.
JEGP   *Journal of English and Germanic Philology.*
Lucas   F. L. Lucas, *The Complete Works of John Webster*, 4 vols. (1927).
MLR   *The Modern Language Review.*
N & Q   *Notes and Queries.*
NS   New Series.
OED   *Oxford English Dictionary.*
PMLA   *Publications of the Modern Language Association of America.*
PQ   *Philological Quarterly.*
SB   *Studies in Bibliography.*
s.d.   stage direction.
Shirley   Frances A. Shirley, *John Webster: The Devil's Law-Case*, Regents Renaissance Drama Series (London, 1972).
s.p.   speech prefix.
Tilley   M. P. Tilley, *A Dictionary of the Proverbs in England in the Sixteenth and Seventeenth Centuries* (Ann Arbor, 1950).

FURTHER READING

THE FOLLOWING BOOKS and articles have made valuable contributions to the study of John Webster and *The Devil's Law-Case*; unless otherwise stated, the place of publication of books is London.

Charles Lamb, *Specimens of English Dramatic Poets, who lived about the Time of Shakespeare: with notes* (1808).

Rupert Brooke, *John Webster and the Elizabethan Drama* (1916).

Clifford Leech, *John Webster: A Critical Study* (1951).

J. R. Brown, 'The Printing of John Webster's Plays' – 3 parts: *SB*, V, 117–40; VIII, 113–28; XV, 57–69 (1954; 1956; 1962).

R. W. Dent, *John Webster's Borrowing* (Berkeley and Los Angeles, 1960).

Fernand Lagarde, *John Webster*, Publications de la Faculté des Lettres et Sciences Humaines de Toulouse, Série A, Tome 7, 2 vols (Toulouse, 1968).

D. C. Gunby, '*The Devil's Law-Case*: An Interpretation', *MLR*, LXIII (1968), 545–58.

G. K. and S. K. Hunter, edd., *John Webster*, Penguin Critical Anthologies (Harmondsworth, 1969).

Brian Morris, ed., *John Webster*, Mermaid Critical Commentaries (1970).

The Deuils Law-case.

OR,

When VVomen goe to Law, the Deuill is full of Businesse.

A new Tragecomædy.

The true and perfect Copie from the Originall.

As it was approouedly well Acted by her Maiesties Seruants.

Written by IOHN WEBSTER.

Non quam diu, sed quam bene.

LONDON,
Printed by *A. M.* for *Iohn Grismand*, and are
to be sold at his Shop in Pauls Alley at the
Signe of the Gunne. 1623.

2 **

10 *Non quam diu, sed quam bene* '[With life, as with a play] it is not a
matter of how long, but of how good it is' (Seneca, *Epistles*, 77,
20)

---

8 *her Maiesties Seruants* the dramatic company, formerly Worcester's
Men, patronized by King James's consort, Queen Anne, from 1603
until her death in 1619. Having played at the Red Bull theatre *c*. 1606–17
they were known in London, between 1619 and their disbandment in
1622, as the Red Bull (Revels) Company and in the provinces as the
Late Queen Anne's Servants.
12 *A.M.* Augustine Mathewes, a printer (fl. 1619–53); *Iohn Grismand*,
printer and bookseller (fl. 1618–38).

The Scene, **NAPLES**

THE ACTORS' NAMES

ROMELIO, *a Merchant*
CONTARINO, *a Nobleman*
CRISPIANO, *a Civil Lawyer* [*from Seville*]
ERCOLE, *a Knight of Malta*
ARIOSTO, *an Advocate*
PROSPERO
JULIO [*Crispiano's son*]
[BAPTISTA]
A CAPUCHIN
CONTILUPO [*a spruce lawyer*]
SANITONELLA [*a lawyer's clerk*]

LEONORA [*mother of Romelio and Jolenta*]
JOLENTA
[WINIFRED,] *a Waiting Woman*
[ANGIOLELLA, *a Nun*]

[TWO SURGEONS; JUDGES; LAWYERS; BELLMEN; REGISTER OF THE COURT;
MARSHAL; HERALD; SERVANTS]

---

2 CONTARINO? from Italian *contare*, to count, to reckon (Florio,
  Queen Anna's New World of Words, 1611)
3 CRISPIANO? from Italian *crispino*, crisped, curled (ibid.)
10 *spruce* smart, but used (IV. i, 71 s.d.) in a pejorative sense

---

4 ERCOLE, *a Knight of Malta* i.e., one of the Knights Hospitaler of St John
  of Jerusalem, vowed to poverty, chastity, and obedience and sworn to
  fight for the Christian faith, to do justice, defend the oppressed, pro-
  tect widows and orphans, and persecute the Mohammedans: see G. K.
  Hunter, 'The Theology of Marlowe's *The Jew of Malta*', *Journal of
  the Warburg and Courtauld Institutes*, XXVII (1964), 229. Though there
  are frequent references in the play to war against the Turks, Webster
  does not keep all the implications of Ercole's vocation as a Knight of
  Malta in mind, as these knights were monastic soldiers.
9 A CAPUCHIN The order of Capuchins had originally separated itself from
  the main body of the Franciscans about 1528 so that it might return
  to the strict austerity of St Francis. It was not established as an in-
  dependent order till 1619.
16 BELLMEN see II. iii, 72 n.

3

TO THE RIGHT WORTHY, AND ALL-ACCOMPLISHED GENTLEMAN, SIR THOMAS FINCH, KNIGHT BARONET.

Sir, let it not appear strange, that I do aspire to your patronage. Things that taste of any goodness, love to be sheltered near   5
goodness. Nor do I flatter in this (which I hate), only touch at the original copy of your virtues. Some of my other works, as *The White Devil, The Duchess of Malfi, Guise*, and others, you have formerly seen; I present this humbly to kiss your hands, and to find your allowance. Nor do I much doubt it, knowing   10
the greatest of the Cæsars, have cheerfully entertained less poems than this: and had I thought it unworthy, I had not inquired after so worthy a patronage. Yourself I understand, to be all courtesy. I doubt not therefore of your acceptance, but resolve, that my election is happy. For which favour done   15
me, I shall ever rest

Your Worship's humbly devoted,
JOHN WEBSTER.

12 *poems* dramatic poems
15 *resolve* am assured; am convinced *election* choice

---

2 *Sir Thomas Finch, Knight Baronet*. In 1623 Dame Elizabeth Finch, widow of Sir Moyle Finch, Bart., in consideration of the services of her father, Sir Thomas Heneage, Vice-Chamberlain of the household of Elizabeth I and Chancellor of the Duchy of Lancaster, who died in 1595, was created Viscountess of Maidstone and, in 1628, Countess of Winchilsea, the earldom being restricted to her male heirs. Sir Thomas Finch, her third son, knighted 1609, succeeded his brother as third baronet *c.* 1619. In 1634 he succeeded his mother to become Earl of Winchilsea. Gervase Markham and W. Sampson dedicated their tragedy of *Herod and Antipater*, also performed by Queen Anne's Servants, to Sir Thomas Finch in 1622 and he was the dedicatee of poems by William Slatyer, Humphry Mill, and Mary Fage.
8 *Guise* see above, pp. vii–viii.
11–12 *the greatest . . . than this* cf. Epistle Dedicatory of *The Duchess of Malfi* ll. 19–22.

TO THE JUDICIOUS READER.

I hold it, in these kind of poems, with that of Horace, *Sapientia prima, stultitia caruisse*, to be free from those vices, which proceed from ignorance; of which I take it, this play will ingeniously acquit itself. I do chiefly therefore expose it   5
to the judicious. *Locus est, & pluribus umbris*, others have leave to sit down, and read it, who come unbidden. But to these, should a man present them with the most excellent music, it would delight them no more, than *Auriculas citharæ collecta sorde dolentes*. I will not further insist upon the approvement of   10
it, for I am so far from praising myself, that I have not given way to divers of my friends, whose unbegged commendatory verses offered themselves to do me service in the front of this poem. A great part of the grace of this (I confess) lay in action; yet can no action ever be gracious, where the decency   15
of the language, and ingenious structure of the scene, arrive not to make up a perfect harmony. What I have failed of this, you that have approved my other works, (when you have read this) tax me of. For the rest, *Non ego ventosæ plebis, suffragia venor*.   20

2 *that of* that saying of
3 *Sapientia prima, stultitia caruisse* 'The first part of wisdom is to be without stupidity' (Horace, *Epistles*, I, i, 41–2)
5 *ingeniously* cleverly, sagaciously
6 *Locus est, & pluribus umbris* 'There is room, and [also] for many shadows [i.e., hangers-on or uninvited guests]' (Horace, *Epistles*, I, v, 28)
9–10 *Auriculas citharæ collecta sorde dolentes* '[It would give them no more pleasure than] the music of citherns to ears afflicted by collected dirt' (Horace, *Epistles*, I, ii, 53)
19–20 *Non ego ventosæ plebis, suffragia venor* 'I do not seek the applause of the fickle multitude' (Horace, *Epistles*, I, xix, 37)

THE DEVIL'S LAW-CASE
OR,
WHEN WOMEN GO TO LAW, THE DEVIL
IS FULL OF BUSINESS

[Act I, Scene i]

Enter ROMELIO *and* PROSPERO

PROSPERO
    You have shown a world of wealth; I did not think
    There had been a merchant lived in Italy
    Of half your substance.
ROMELIO   I'll give the King of Spain
    Ten thousand ducats yearly, and discharge
    My yearly custom. The Hollanders scarce trade   5
    More generally than I: my factors' wives
    Wear chaperons of velvet, and my scriveners
    Merely through my employment, grow so rich,
    They build their palaces and belvederes
    With musical water-works. Never in my life   10
    Had I a loss at sea. They call me on th'Exchange
    The Fortunate Young Man and make great suit
    To venture with me. Shall I tell you sir,
    Of a strange confidence in my way of trading?
    I reckon it as certain as the gain   15
    In erecting a lottery.
PROSPERO   I pray sir, what do you think
    Of Signior Baptista's estate?
ROMELIO   A mere beggar:
    He's worth some fifty thousand ducats.
PROSPERO   Is not that well?

---

  5 *custom* import duty
  6 *More generally* in more different parts of the world
  7 *chaperons* French hoods, originally worn by nobles, but adopted
    by ladies of fashion in the 16th century
  9 *belvederes* raised turrets on a roof; summer houses built on heights
    commanding a fine view
10 *musical water-works* streams or fountains contrived to produce
    music from mechanical birds
12 *Fortunate Young Man* ed. (fortunate Youngman Q)

The first scene takes place outside Leonora's house.

ROMELIO

    How well? For a man to be melted to snow-water,
    With toiling in the world from three and twenty   20
    Till threescore, for poor fifty thousand ducats.

PROSPERO

    To your estate 'tis little I confess:
    You have the spring-tide of gold.

ROMELIO   Faith, and for silver,
    Should I not send it packing to th'East Indies,
    We should have a glut on't.   25

Enter SERVANT

SERVANT

    Here's the great lord Contarino.

PROSPERO   Oh, I know
    His business; he's a suitor to your sister.

ROMELIO

    Yes sir, but to you,
    As my most trusted friend, I utter it,
    I will break the alliance.

PROSPERO   You are ill advised then;   30
    There lives not a completer gentleman
    In Italy, nor of a more ancient house.

ROMELIO

    What tell you me of gentry? 'Tis nought else
    But a superstitious relic of time past:
    And sift it to the true worth, it is nothing   35
    But ancient riches: and in him, you know,
    They are pitifully in the wane; he makes his colour
    Of visiting us so often, to sell land,

---

37 *colour* pretext, excuse

19–20 cf. Pierre Matthieu, *Henry the Fourth*: 'Your greatnesses are but
    heapes of snow, which we see melt into water . . .' (Sig. Xx3ᵛ) (Dent,
    p. 272).
23 *spring-tide* the tide occurring in the days following the new and full
    moons, when the maximum high water-level is reached; hence, figura-
    tively, a copious quantity
33–4 The source of this phrase, also used by Webster in the Epistle
    Dedicatory to *The Duchess of Malfi*, ll. 14–15, is Overbury's character
    'A Wife' (1614): '*Gentry* is but a *relique* of Time past' (Dent, p. 290).
35–6 *it is . . . riches* The phrase is taken directly from Burghley's *Certaine
    Precepts* (1617), though the idea it contains is to be found in Guazzo,
    Segar, Breton, and other writers: see Dent, p. 290.

And thinks if he can gain my sister's love,
To recover the treble value.
PROSPERO   Sure he loves her   40
Entirely, and she deserves it.
ROMELIO   Faith, though she were
Crook'd-shouldered, having such a portion,
She would have noble suitors; but truth is,
I would wish my noble venturer take heed,
It may be whiles he hopes to catch a gilthead   45
He may draw up a gudgeon.

Enter CONTARINO

PROSPERO   He's come. Sir, I will leave you.
                [*Exeunt* PROSPERO *and* SERVANT]
CONTARINO
I sent you the evidence of the piece of land
I motioned to you for the sale.
ROMELIO   Yes.
CONTARINO
Has your counsel perused it?
ROMELIO   Not yet, my lord. Do you
Intend to travel?
CONTARINO   No.
ROMELIO   Oh then you lose   50
That which makes man most absolute.
CONTARINO   Yet I have heard
Of divers, that in passing of the Alps,
Have but exchanged their virtues at dear rate
For others' vices.
ROMELIO   Oh my lord, lie not idle;

42 *Crook'd-shouldered* hunchbacked
45 *gilthead* fish with gold spots or lines on its head
46 *gudgeon* tiny fish used as bait
47 *evidence* title-deeds
48 *motioned* proposed
50 *lose* ed. (loose Q)
51 *absolute* complete
54 *others'* ed. (other Q): see Textual Appendix A

52-4 *in passing . . . vices* another phrase borrowed from Burghley's *Cer-*
taine Precepts: 'Suffer not your Sonnes to passe the *Alpes*: for they
shall exchange for theyr forraine trauell (vnlesse they goe better forti-
fied) but others vices for thyr owne vertues, . . .' (Dent, p. 291).

The chiefest action for a man of great spirit   55
Is never to be out of action: we should think
The soul was never put into the body,
Which has so many rare and curious pieces
Of mathematical motion, to stand still.
Virtue is ever sowing of her seeds: 60
In the trenches for the soldier; in the wakeful study
For the scholar; in the furrows of the sea
For men of our profession; of all which
Arise and spring up honour. Come, I know
You have some noble great design in hand,   65
That you levy so much money.

CONTARINO   Sir, I'll tell you:
The greatest part of it I mean to employ
In payment of my debts, and the remainder
Is like to bring me into greater bonds,
As I aim it.

ROMELIO   How sir?

CONTARINO   I intend it   70
For the charge of my wedding.

ROMELIO   Are you to be married, my lord?

CONTARINO
Yes sir; and I must now entreat your pardon,
That I have concealed from you a business,
Wherein you had at first been called to counsel,
But that I thought it a less fault in friendship,   75
To engage myself thus far without your knowledge,
Than to do it against your will: another reason
Was, that I would not publish to the world,
Nor have it whispered scarce, what wealthy voyage
I went about, till I had got the mine   80
In mine own possession.

---

59 *mathematical* with mathematical accuracy: cf *The White Devil*,
    I. ii, 89–90
71 *charge* expense
79 *scarce* scarcely

55–9 Lucas first indicated a source for these lines in Sidney's *Arcadia*, I,
    ix, but Dent (p. 291) suggests a supplementary source, also used by
    Dekker for *The Seven Deadly Sinnes of London* (1606).
75–7 from Sidney's *Arcadia*, I, xiii: 'This made me determine with my
    self, (thinking it a lesse fault in friendship to do a thing without your
    knowledge, then against your wil) to take this secret course' (Dent. p. 292).

ROMELIO   You are dark to me yet.

CONTARINO
I'll now remove the cloud. Sir, your sister and I
Are vowed each other's, and there only wants
Her worthy mother's and your fair consents
To style it marriage: this is a way,   85
Not only to make a friendship, but confirm it
For our posterities. How do you look upon't?

ROMELIO
Believe me sir, as on the principal column
To advance our house: why, you bring honour with you,
Which is the soul of wealth. I shall be proud   90
To live to see my little nephews ride
O'th'upper hand of their uncles, and the daughters
Be ranked by heralds at solemnities
Before the mother: all this derived
From your nobility. Do not blame me sir,   95
If I be taken with't exceedingly:
For this same honour, with us citizens,
Is a thing we are mainly fond of, especially
When it comes without money, which is very seldom.
But as you do perceive my present temper,   100
Be sure I am yours, [aside] – fired with scorn and laughter,
At your over-confident purpose, – and no doubt,
My mother will be of your mind.

                                          Exit ROMELIO
CONTARINO   'Tis my hope sir.
I do observe how this Romelio
Has very worthy parts, were they not blasted   105
By insolent vain-glory: there rests now
The mother's approbation to the match,
Who is a woman of that state and bearing,
Though she be city-born, both in her language,

98 *mainly* exceedingly
105 *parts* abilities
108 *that state* that kind of state

---

81 *You are dark to me* i.e., 'Your meaning is dark to me': Romelio is
pretending not to understand, but he knows very well what Contarino
is about, as he has told Prospero (see above, ll. 37–46).
103 s.d.: after l. 103b in Dyce, Hazlitt, and Lucas. Q's positioning, retained here, accords with Romelio's withdrawal—presumably to summon
Leonora—as soon as he has finished speaking. Contarino's answer may
be addressed to his retreating figure.

Her garments, and her table, she excels   110
Our ladies of the court: she goes not gaudy,
Yet I have seen her wear one diamond,
Would have bought twenty gay ones out of their clothes,
And some of them, without the greater grace,
Out of their honesties.

Enter LEONORA

       She comes, I will try   115
How she stands affected to me, without relating
My contract with her daughter.
LEONORA
Sir, you are nobly welcome, and presume
You are in a place that's wholly dedicated
To your service.
CONTARINO   I am ever bound to you   120
For many special favours.
LEONORA   Sir, your fame
Renders you most worthy of it.
CONTARINO   It could never have got
A sweeter air to fly in, than your breath.
LEONORA
You have been strange a long time; you are weary
Of our unseasonable time of feeding: 125
Indeed th'Exchange Bell makes us dine so late;
I think the ladies of the court from us
Learn to lie so long abed.
CONTARINO
They have a kind of Exchange among them too;
Marry, unless it be to hear of news, I take it,   130

110 *she excels* that she excels
111 *gaudy* gaudily dressed
114 *without the greater grace* 'into the bargain (i.e., with regarding it as
  an extra favour') (Lucas)
115 *honesties* chastities; s.d.: opposite l. 115b in Q, Lucas; after l. 117
  in Dyce and Hazlitt
118 *presume* may presume
124 *strange* distant

---

126 *th'Exchange Bell* announced the time when the Exchange was open to
  merchants for business. In London in the early 17th century this was
  between 11 a.m. and noon. Thus merchants seldom took their morning
  meal—more properly breakfast than lunch—before noon. Court
  ladies who, rising late, breakfasted at the same hour, could be said to
  imitate them.

Theirs is like the New Burse, thinly furnished
With tires and new fashions. I have a suit to you.

LEONORA

I would not have you value it the less,
If I say, ' 'Tis granted already'.

CONTARINO   You are all bounty.
'Tis to bestow your picture on me.

LEONORA   Oh sir,   135
Shadows are coveted in summer, and with me,
'Tis fall o'th' leaf.

CONTARINO   You enjoy the best of time;
This latter spring of yours shows in my eye
More fruitful and more temperate withal,
Than that whose date is only limited   140
By the music of the cuckoo.

LEONORA   Indeed sir, I dare tell you,
My looking-glass is a true one, and as yet
It does not terrify me. Must you have my picture?

CONTARINO

So please you, lady, and I shall preserve it
As a most choice object.   145

LEONORA

You will enjoin me to a strange punishment.
With what a compelled face a woman sits
While she is drawing! I have noted divers
Either to feign smiles, or suck in the lips

132   *tires* articles of dress
136   *Shadows* usual meaning; pictures
138   *latter spring* late or second spring, coming comparatively late in
       life
147   *compelled* forced; unnatural
148   *drawing* i.e., being drawn or painted

---

131   *the New Burse* The New Exchange in the Strand, London was opened in
      1609 by James I. The Old Exchange, founded by the Elizabethan
      merchant Sir Thomas Gresham, 42 years earlier, was situated in
      Cornhill. There were shops for millinery and other items of female
      fashion on either side of the New Exchange, but trade in them was
      slack at first and the shops were therefore *thinly furnished*, i.e., poorly
      stocked.
140-1   limited by the time when the cuckoo is in England, i.e., April to
      July. Contarino's words also imply the usual relationship between
      'cuckoo' and 'cuckold'.
142   *My looking-glass is a true one*, i.e., 'it does not flatter me': cf. *The Duchess
      of Malfi*, I. ii, 126-7.

To have a little mouth; ruffle the cheeks   150
To have the dimple seen, and so disorder
The face with affectation, at next sitting
It has not been the same; I have known others
Have lost the entire fashion of their face,
In half an hour's sitting.
CONTARINO   How?
LEONORA   In hot weather,   155
The painting on their face has been so mellow,
They have left the poor man harder work by half,
To mend the copy he wrought by: but indeed,
If ever I would have mine drawn to th'life,
I would have a painter steal it, at such a time   160
I were devoutly kneeling at my prayers;
There is then a heavenly beauty in't, the soul
Moves in the superficies.
CONTARINO   Excellent lady,
Now you teach beauty a preservative,
More than 'gainst fading colours; and your judgement   165
Is perfect in all things.
LEONORA   Indeed sir, I am a widow,
And want the addition to make it so:
For man's experience has still been held
Woman's best eyesight. I pray sir tell me,
You are about to sell a piece of land   170
To my son, I hear.
CONTARINO   'Tis truth.
LEONORA   Now I could rather wish,

---

150 *ruffle* disarrange (? by puffing out: cf. Florio, op. cit.: '*Ruffo*, a
    belching, a rasping, a breaking of winde vpward')
154 *fashion* appearance
156 *painting* cosmetic; *mellow* soft (and therefore running)
163 *superficies* surface
166 *perfect* usual meaning; complete
167 *addition* that which needs to be added to make it complete, i.e., a
    husband's experience
168 *still* always

168-9 from *Arcadia*, III. v where the widow Cecropia recommends marriage
    to her niece: 'mans experience is womans best eie-sight' (Dent, p. 292).
171-4 Between 1617 and 1623 James I issued three proclamations exhorting
    country nobility and gentry to stay at home and not come up to London.
    He blamed the pride of their womenfolk for their resorting to London:
    see Lucas, II, 325.

That noblemen would ever live i'th' country,
Rather than make their visits up to th'city
About such business. Oh sir, noble houses
Have no such goodly prospects any way,   175
As into their own land: the decay of that,
Next to their begging church-land, is a ruin
Worth all men's pity. Sir, I have forty thousand crowns
Sleep in my chest, shall waken when you please,
And fly to your commands. Will you stay supper?   180

CONTARINO
I cannot, worthy lady.

LEONORA
I would not have you come hither sir, to sell,
But to settle your estate. I hope you understand
Wherefore I make this proffer: so I leave you.
                                    Exit LEON[ORA]

CONTARINO
What a treasury have I pearched! 'I hope   185
You understand wherefore I make this proffer'.
She has got some intelligence, how I intend to marry
Her daughter, and ingenuously perceived,
That by her picture, which I begged of her,
I meant the fair Jolenta. Here's a letter   190
Which gives express charge, not to visit her
Till midnight: [*reads*] *Fail not to come, for 'tis a business*
That concerns both our honours.
                    Yours in danger to be lost, Jolenta.
'Tis a strange injunction; what should be the business?   195
She is not changed I hope. I'll thither straight:
For women's resolutions in such deeds,
Like bees, light oft on flowers, and oft on weeds.   *Exit*

175 *prospects* expectations; views
179 *Sleep* which sleep
180 *stay* wait for
185 *pearched!* ed. (pearch'd. Q; [On] . . . perch'd! Dyce; perch'd on!
      Hazlitt; pearch'd! Lucas) pierced
188 *ingenuously* ingeniously
192–3 italics: ed.
196 *straight* immediately

177 *begging church-land* The greedy appropriation of church-land at the
      time of the Reformation was supposed to have brought retribution on
      those responsible: see Lucas, II, 325.

[Act I, Scene ii]

Enter ERCOLE, ROMELIO, JOLENTA

ROMELIO
  Oh sister, come, the tailor must to work,
  To make your wedding clothes.
JOLENTA   The tomb-maker,
  To take measure of my coffin.
ROMELIO   Tomb-maker?
  Look you, the King of Spain greets you. [*He gives her a paper*]
JOLENTA   What does this mean,
  Do you serve process on me?
ROMELIO   Process, come,   5
  You would be witty now.
JOLENTA   Why, what's this, I pray?
ROMELIO
  Infinite grace to you: it is a letter
  From His Catholic Majesty, for the commends
  Of this gentleman for your husband.
JOLENTA   In good season:
  I hope he will not have my allegiance stretched   10
  To the undoing of myself.
ROMELIO
  Undo yourself? He does proclaim him here –
JOLENTA
  Not for a traitor, does he?
ROMELIO   You are not mad?
  For one of the noblest gentlemen.
JOLENTA   Yet kings many times
  Know merely but men's outsides; was this commendation 15

---

5 *process* legal summons
7 *grace* manifestation of a favour
8 *commends* commendation
9 *In good season* in due time
12 *proclaim* make an official announcement about; denounce

The scene is probably set within Leonora's house and therefore acted on the
inner stage.
  4 s.d. 'I suppose Romelio hands his sister, as if it were a letter addressed
    to her in person, the commission in which the King of Spain names
    Ercole the commander of thirty galleys. The document may well have
    begun with a general official greeting to all whom the appointment
    might concern . . .' (Lucas, II, 326).

Voluntary, think you?

ROMELIO   Voluntary: what mean you by that?

JOLENTA

Why I do not think but he begged it of the king,
And it may fortune to be out of's way:
Some better suit, that would have stood his lordship
In far more stead. Letters of commendations!   20
Why 'tis reported that they are grown stale,
When places fall i'th'university.
I pray you return his pass: for to a widow
That longs to be a courtier, this paper
May do knight's service.   25

ERCOLE

Mistake not, excellent mistress, these commends
Express, His Majesty of Spain has given me
Both addition of honour, as you may perceive
By my habit, and a place here to command
O'er thirty galleys; this your brother shows,   30
As wishing that you would be partner
In my good fortune.

ROMELIO   I pray come hither,
Have I any interest in you?

JOLENTA   You are my brother.

ROMELIO

I would have you then use me with that respect,
You may still keep me so, and to be swayed   35
In this main business of life, which wants
Greatest consideration, your marriage,
By my direction. Here's a gentleman –

21 *stale* hackneyed; out-of-date
22 *fall* fall vacant
23 *pass* testimonial (Lucas)
24 *courtier* frequenter of the court
25 *knight's service* good and loyal service: cf. yeoman service
28 *addition* rank, title
33 *interest in* personal influence with
36 *main* serious, important

18–20 Jolenta suggests that though Ercole has been successful in obtaining
the letter of commendation from the king, which is in fact useless as a
means of furthering his amatory suit, since she is unimpressed by it,
he may find himself also unsuccessful when he wishes the king to
grant him a suit which would be more helpful to him.

JOLENTA
  Sir, I have often told you,
  I am so little my own to dispose that way,   40
  That I can never be his.
ROMELIO   Come, too much light
  Makes you moon-eyed; are you in love with title?
  I will have a herald, whose continual practice
  Is all in pedigree, come a-wooing to you,
  Or an antiquary in old buskins.
ERCOLE   Sir, you have done me   45
  The mainest wrong that e'er was offered
  To a gentleman of my breeding.
ROMELIO   Why sir?
ERCOLE   You have led me
  With a vain confidence, that I should marry
  Your sister; have proclaimed it to my friends,
  Employed the greatest lawyers of out state   50
  To settle her a jointure, and the issue
  Is, that I must become ridiculous
  Both to my friends and enemies. I will leave you,
  Till I call to you for a strict account
  Of your unmanly dealing.
ROMELIO   Stay my lord.   55
  [*Aside, to* JOLENTA] Do you long to have my throat cut? –
    Good my lord,
  Stay but a little, till I have removed
  This court-mist from her eyes, till I wake her
  From this dull sleep, wherein she'll dream herself
  To a deformed beggar. [*To* JOLENTA] You would marry   60
  The great lord Contarino –

Enter LEONORA

LEONORA   Contarino

45 *buskins* calf- or knee-length leather boots, out of fashion by the
    early 17th century
46 *mainest* most serious
49 *have* i.e., I have
51 *issue* result
61 *Contarino* – Dyce, Hazlitt (*Contarino.* Q, Lucas)

---

42 *moon-eyed* originally a farrier's term, applied to animals suffering from
    an intermittent blindness that was attributed to the moon's influence;
    by extension it become applied to mental blindness (Lucas).
58 *court-mist* a dazzling haze emanating from the court, and from the
    courtier Contarino, which is causing Jolenta's moon-blindness.

Were you talking of? He lost last night at dice
Five thousand ducats; and when that was gone,
Set at one throw a lordship, that twice trebled
The former loss.   65

ROMELIO
And that flew after.

LEONORA   And most carefully
Carried the gentleman in his caroche
To a lawyer's chamber, there most legally
To put him in possession: was this wisdom?

ROMELIO
Oh yes, their credit in the way of gaming   70
Is the main thing they stand on, that must be paid,
Though the brewer bawl for's money; and this lord
Does she prefer i'th' way of marriage,
Before our choice here, noble Ercole.

LEONORA [to JOLENTA]
You'll be advised I hope. Know for your sakes   75
I married, that I might have children;
And for your sakes, if you'll be ruled by me,
I will never marry again. Here's a gentleman
Is noble, rich, well-featured, but 'bove all,
He loves you entirely; his intents are aimed   80
For an expedition 'gainst the Turk,
Which makes the contract cannot be delayed.

JOLENTA
Contract? You must do this without my knowledge;
Give me some potion to make me mad,
And happily, not knowing what I speak,   85

67 *caroche* large coach used by the noble and wealthy
69 *possession* i.e., of the lordship
71 *stand on* insist on   74 *choice here*, ed. (choyce. Here Q)
82 *makes* makes it that
85 *happily* haply, perhaps

62–5 i.e., having lost 5,000 ducats, Contarino staked an estate worth 30,000
    ducats against a single throw of the dice; and he lost that, too.
72 *the brewer* i.e., a mere tradesman, as opposed to the gentlemen with
    whom Contarino plays at dice.
82 *contract* There was considerable contemporary debate about the validity
    of this kind of marriage contract; for fuller discussion see the following
    articles, which are not always in agreement: D. P. Harding, 'Elizabethan
    Betrothals and *Measure for Measure*', *JEGP*, XLIX (1950), 139–58 and
    Ernest Schanzer, 'The Marriage Contracts in *Measure for Measure*',
    Shakespeare Survey 13 (1960), 81–9.

I may then consent to't.

ROMELIO   Come, you are mad already,
And I shall never hear you speak good sense,
Till you name him for husband.

ERCOLE   Lady, I will do
A manly office for you, I will leave you
To the freedom of your own soul; may it move whither   90
Heaven and you please.

JOLENTA   Now you express yourself
Most nobly.

ROMELIO   Stay sir, what do you mean to do?

LEONORA [kneeling]
Hear me, if thou dost marry Contarino,
All the misfortune that did ever dwell
In a parent's curse, light on thee!

ERCOLE   Oh rise lady,   95
Certainly heaven never intended kneeling
To this fearful purpose.

JOLENTA
Your imprecation has undone me for ever.

ERCOLE
Give me your hand.

JOLENTA   No sir.

ROMELIO   Give't me then: [takes her hand]
Oh what rare workmanship have I seen this   100
To finish with your needle, what excellent music
Have these struck upon the viol! Now I'll teach
A piece of art.

JOLENTA   Rather, a damnable cunning,
To have me go about to give't away,
Without consent of my soul.

ROMELIO   Kiss her my lord,   105
If crying had been regarded, maidenheads
Had ne'er been lost; at least some appearance of crying,
As an April shower i'th' sunshine. [ERCOLE embraces JOLENTA]

95 thee! ed. (thee. Q)   102 these i.e., Jolenta's fingers

93–5 A parent's curse was particularly abhorred by the Elizabethans and
Jacobeans—see M. C. Bradbrook, 'Two Notes upon Webster', MLR,
XLII (1947), 281–94. Cornelia's curse on Vittoria, pronounced in
The White Devil, I. ii, 282–9, is immediately feared by Brachiano
(I. ii, 294–6) and is, indeed, fulfilled in the end of the play.
102 ff. cf. The White Devil, V. ii, 146–92 where Flamineo teaches Brach-
iano how to woo his sister Vittoria.

LEONORA   She is yours.

ROMELIO
Nay, continue your station, and deal you in dumb show;
Kiss this doggedness out of her.

LEONORA   To be contracted   110
In tears, is but fashionable.

ROMELIO   Yet suppose
That they were hearty?

LEONORA   Virgins must seem unwilling.

ROMELIO
Oh what else? And you remember, we observe
The like in greater ceremonies than these contracts,
At the consecration of prelates, they use ever   115
Twice to say nay, and take it.

JOLENTA   Oh brother!

ROMELIO
Keep your possession, you have the door by th'ring,
That's livery and seisin in England; but my lord,
Kiss that tear from her lip, you'll find the rose

109 *continue your station* hold your position: 'the metaphor is apparently of a
    moveable "pageant" or stage on wheels, such as was used in the English
    mystery-cycles. The "stations" are the places where the pageants, in
    their procession through the town, stop and perform their "turn"'
    (Lucas, II, 327). Thus Ercole is told not to move away from Jolenta,
    but to maintain his station beside her; *deal you in dumb show* then,
    continuing the acting metaphor, he is told to perform his part without
    speaking.
111–12 i.e., 'What would happen if virgins were cheerful at the prospect of
    marriage?'
115–16 It was customary for clerics to decline the offer of bishoprics with
    the phrase 'Nolo episcopari' at least twice. Lucas, II, 327, says that
    there is little evidence for this custom, but is able to substantiate it by
    reference to Dryden's *The Kind Keeper, or Mr. Limberham*, while
    Dent (p. 293) points to a possible source in Sir Thomas More's *Richard
    the Thirde*.
117–18 There is an allusion here to the feudal form of conveyancing estates,
    called 'feoffment with livery (delivery) and seisin' (possession) whereby
    the feoffer would give the feofee the ring or latch of a house which was
    being conveyed (Lucas, II, 327–8). Lucas points out a similar meta-
    phorical use of the phrase in Marston's *Antonio and Mellida* and Dent
    (p. 293) finds a closer parallel in Barrey's *Ram-Alley* (1611), where a
    lawyer speaks:
        Short tale to make I fingered haue your daughter:
        I haue tane liuery and seazon of the wench.
    At l. 116 Lucas has the s.d. [*He seizes her hand and lays it in Ercole's*],
    but it is possible that Ercole still has an arm round her (see above, l. 108).

The sweeter for the dew.

JOLENTA   Bitter as gall.   120

ROMELIO

Ay, ay, all you women,
Although you be of never so low stature,
Have gall in you most abundant; it exceeds
Your brains by two ounces. I was saying somewhat;
Oh do but observe i'th'city, and you'll find   125
The thriftiest bargains that were ever made,
What a deal of wrangling ere they could be brought
To an upshot.

LEONORA

Great persons do not ever come together –

ROMELIO

With revelling faces, nor is it necessary   130
They should; the strangeness and unwillingness
Wears the greater state, and gives occasion that
The people may buzz and talk of't, though the bells
Be tongue-tied at the wedding.

LEONORA

And truly I have heard say,   135
To be a little strange to one another,
Will keep your longing fresh.

ROMELIO   Ay, and make you beget
More children when y'are married: some doctors
Are of that opinion. You see my lord, we are merry
At the contract; your sport is to come hereafter.   140

ERCOLE [to JOLENTA]

I will leave you, excellent lady, and withal
Leave a heart with you so entirely yours,
That I protest, had I the least of hope
To enjoy you, though I were to wait the time
That scholars do in taking their degree   145
In the noble Arts, 'twere nothing; howsoe'er,
He parts from you, that will depart from life,
To do you any service, and so humbly

127 *ere* before
128 *upshot* conclusion   132 *state* appearance of nobility
133 *buzz* spread as a rumour, with whispering or busy talk
134 *tongue-tied* (i) literally, with their clappers tied; (ii) unable to make a
     sound

144–5 *to wait . . . degree* The usual period of study for an Arts degree at this
       time was seven years.

I take my leave.
JOLENTA   Sir, I will pray for you.   *Exit* ERCOLE
ROMELIO
Why that's well, 'twill make your prayer complete,   150
To pray for your husband.
JOLENTA   Husband?
LEONORA   This is
The happiest hour that I ever arrived at.   [*Exit*]
ROMELIO
Husband, ay, husband: come you peevish thing,
Smile me a thank for the pains I have ta'en.
JOLENTA
I hate myself for being thus enforced,   155
You may soon judge then what I think of you
Which are the cause of it.

Enter [WINIFRED, *the*] *waiting-woman*

ROMELIO
You lady of the laundry, come hither.
WINIFRED   Sir?
ROMELIO
Look as you love your life, you have an eye
Upon your mistress: I do henceforth bar her   160
All visitants. I do hear there are bawds abroad,
That bring cut-works, and mantoons, and convey letters
To such young gentlewomen, and there are others
That deal in corn-cutting, and fortune-telling:
Let none of these come at her, on your life,   165
Nor Deuce-ace, the wafer-woman, that prigs abroad

149 s.d.: opposite l. 149a in Q
150–1 cf. I. i, 166–7   153 *peevish* headstrong
158 *lady of the laundry* i.e., laundress, reputedly of easy virtue: cf.
     The White Devil, IV. i, 91
158 s.p. *et seq.* WINIFRED ed. (*Wayt.* Q)
162 *cut-works* a kind of open work made by cutting out or stamping,
     used in dress material in Italy in the late 16th and early 17th
     centuries: cf. *The White Devil*, I. i, 51; *mantoons* large mantles
166 *prigs* (i) steals; (ii) rides about: see A. Harbage, *A Dictionary of the
     Underworld* (1949), *s.v.* 'prig'

155–7 from *Arcadia*, I, i: 'Assure thy selfe, I hate my selfe for being so
     deceived; judge then what I doo thee, for deceiving me' (Dent, p. 294).
166 *Deuce-ace* is a throw in dice which turns up ace on one side and deuce
     on the other. As this is a poor throw it is a suitable nickname for a poor
     woman. A *wafer-woman* sold sweet wafers and other confectionery. 'As a
     class they were notorious go-betweens' (Lucas, II, 328).

With muskmelons, and malakatoons;
Nor the Scotchwoman with the cittern, do you mark;
Nor a dancer by any means, though he ride on's foot-cloth,
Nor a hackney-coachman, if he can speak French.   170
WINIFRED
Why sir?
ROMELIO   By no means: no more words;
Nor the woman with the maribone puddings. I have heard
Strange juggling tricks have been conveyed to a woman
In a pudding: you are apprehensive?
WINIFRED
Oh good sir, I have travelled.
ROMELIO   When you had a bastard,   175
You travelled indeed. But my precious chaperoness,
I trust thee the better for that; for I have heard,
There is no warier keeper of a park,
To prevent stalkers, or your night-walkers,
Than such a man as in his youth has been   180
A most notorious deer-stealer.
WINIFRED   Very well sir,
You may use me at your pleasure.
ROMELIO
By no means Winifred, that were the way
To make thee travel again. Come, be not angry,
I do but jest; thou knowest, wit and a woman   185
Are two very frail things; and so I leave you.   [*Exit*]

167 *muskmelons* oriental melons tasting of musk, a favourite flavour;
    malakatoons the fruit of a peach grafted on to a quince
168 *cittern* a stringed instrument, like a guitar
169 *foot-cloth* an ornamental cloth which covered the horse's back and
    hung down to the ground, considered a sign of dignity: cf. *The
    White Devil*, I. i, 49
172 *maribone puddings* marrow-bone puddings, considered to be
    aphrodisiac
174 *you are apprehensive?* do you understand?
175-6 *travelled* (i) usual meaning; (ii) travailed in childbirth
176 *chaperoness* ? wearer of a chaperon (see I. i, 7 n). The modern
    sense of a chaperone as a female escort to an unmarried lady is not
    recorded in *OED* before 1720
179 *stalkers* deer-stealers; *night-walkers* thieves who prowl at night
182 *use me* (i) usual meaning; (ii) with sexual connotations
185-6 see Textual Appendix A

---

170 *hackney-coachman* From the context it seems likely that this makes some
    joke about hackney = prostitute or bawd.

WINIFRED
  I could weep with you, but 'tis no matter,
  I can do that at any time; I have now
  A greater mind to rail a little. Plague of these
  Unsanctified matches; they make us loathe   190
  The most natural desire our grandam Eve ever left us!
  Force one to marry against their will! Why 'tis
  A more ungodly work, than enclosing the commons.

JOLENTA
  Prithee, peace:
  This is indeed an argument so common,   195
  I cannot think of matter new enough,
  To express it bad enough.

WINIFRED   Here's one I hope
  Will put you out of't.

Enter CONTARINO

CONTARINO   How now, sweet mistress?
  You have made sorrow look lovely of late,
  You have wept.   200

WINIFRED
  She has done nothing else these three days; had you stood
  behind the arras, to have heard her shed so much salt water
  as I have done, you would have thought she had been turned
  fountain.

CONTARINO
  I would fain know the cause can be worthy this   205
  Thy sorrow.

JOLENTA   Reach me the caskanet. I am studying sir,
  To take an inventory of all that's mine.

CONTARINO
  What to do with it lady?

JOLENTA   To make you a deed of gift.

191 *grandam* grandmother   201 *three* Qb (thee Qa)
206 *caskanet* derived from a confusion of carcanet (an ornamental
    jewelled collar) and casket, the word commonly expressed the
    meaning of either in the 17th century: here the latter sense is
    intended

---

193 *enclosing the commons* The enclosing of common land for sheepfarming
    by rich landowners caused great hardship and provoked minor peasants'
    uprisings in the early 17th century: cf. *The White Devil*, I. ii, 91–3.
206 ff. Earlier, Leonora's attitude to Ercole recalls the Duchess of Malfi's
    wooing of Antonio. Here Jolenta directly echoes *The Duchess of Malfi*
    I. ii, 280 ff.

CONTARINO
That's done already; you are all mine.
WINIFRED
Yes, but the devil would fain put in for's share, in likeness of   210
a separation.
JOLENTA
Oh sir, I am bewitched.
CONTARINO   Ha?
JOLENTA   Most certain; I am forespoken
To be married to another: can you ever think
That I shall ever thrive in't? Am I not then bewitched?
All comfort I can teach myself is this,   215
There is a time left for me to die nobly,
When I cannot live so!
CONTARINO   Give me in a word, to whom,
Or by whose means are you thus torn from me?
JOLENTA
By Lord Ercole, my mother, and my brother.
CONTARINO
I'll make his bravery fitter for a grave,   220
Than for a wedding.
JOLENTA   So you will beget
A far more dangerous and strange disease
Out of the cure; you must love him again
For my sake: for the noble Ercole
Had such a true compassion of my sorrow.   225
Hark in your ear, I'll show you his right worthy
Demeanour to me. [*She whispers in his ear, and he embraces her*]
WINIFRED [*aside*]   Oh you pretty ones!
I have seen this lord many a time and oft
Set her in's lap, and talk to her of love

211 *separation* share, portion; divorce *a mensa et thoro*
212 *forespoken* betrothed; bewitched   219 *my* ed. (by Q)
220 *bravery* fine clothes

216–17 from *Arcadia*, III, xxvii: 'for then would be the time to die nobly,
     when you can not live nobly'. The sentiment is also expressed in Seneca's
     Epistles, xvii, 5 (Dent, p. 295).
220–1 from Jonson's *Sejanus*, I, 568–70:
     . . . my sword
     Shall make thy brau'rie fitter for a graue,
     Then for a triumph.   (Dent, p. 295).
221–3 The image here in metaphor anticipates the later action of the play.
     Webster employs the same technique of anticipating action by image
     in the first act of *The Duchess of Malfi*.

So feelingly, I do protest it has made me   230
Run out of myself to think on't: oh sweet-breathed
    monkey!
How they grow together! Well, 'tis my opinion,
He was no woman's friend that did invent
A punishment for kissing.

CONTARINO
If he bear himself so nobly,   235
The manliest office I can do for him,
Is to afford him my pity, since he's like
To fail of so dear a purchase: for your mother,
Your goodness quits her ill; for your brother,
He that vows friendship to a man, and proves   240
A traitor, deserves rather to be hanged,
Than he that counterfeits money; yet for your sake
I must sign his pardon too. Why do you tremble?
Be safe, you are now free from him.

JOLENTA   Oh but sir,
The intermission from a fit of an ague   245
Is grievous: for indeed it doth prepare us,
To entertain torment next morning.

CONTARINO
Why, he's gone to sea.

JOLENTA   But he may return too soon.

CONTARINO
To avoid which, we will instantly be married.

WINIFRED
To avoid which, get you instantly to bed together;   250
Do, and I think no civil lawyer for his fee
Can give you better counsel.

231 *monkey* Q (monkeys Dyce)
238 *dear* expensive; beloved; *purchase* acquisition, prize
239 *quits* acquits; balances

---

231 *sweet-breathed monkey* The idea that the monkey's breath was sweet
    is found in the first Eclogues of *Arcadia* (Lucas, II, 329). Monkeys
    were also notorious for lechery: see *Othello*, III. iii, 409.
232–4 'perhaps an allusion to Cato the Elder who degraded Manilius from
    the Senate for kissing his own wife in the daytime in the presence of
    their daughter (Plutarch, *Cato*, 17)' (Lucas, II, 329–30).
240–2 Dent suggests a possible source for these lines in Guazzo's comment
    on flatterers: 'the Philosopher counteth him worse then a forger of
    monie, for that there can be no friendship, where there is counter-
    feiting' (Dent, pp. 295–6).
244–6 cf. *The Duchess of Malfi*, V. iv, 66–8.

JOLENTA
Fie upon thee, prithee leave us.   [*Exit* WINIFRED]
CONTARINO
Be of comfort, sweet mistress.
JOLENTA
On one condition: we may have no quarrel   255
About this.
CONTARINO   Upon my life, none.
JOLENTA   None,
Upon your honour?
CONTARINO   With whom? With Ercole?
You have delivered him guiltless. With your brother?
He's part of yourself. With your complimental mother?
I use not fight with women. Tomorrow we'll   260
Be married. Let those that would oppose this union
Grow ne'er so subtle, and entangle themselves
In their own work like spiders, while we two
Haste to our noble wishes, and presume
The hinderance of it will breed more delight,   265
As black copartiments shows gold more bright.   *Exeunt*

Finis Actus primus

255 *quarrel* i.e., one resulting in a duel between Contarino and Ercole
     and/or Romelio
259 *complimental* excessively courteous; formal
260 *I use not* I am not accustomed to
266 *copartiments* ornamental, subdivisional parts of a design: e.g.,
     sunken panels in a ceiling: 'Compartimento, *a partition, a compart-*
     ment, a sharing with' (Florio, op. cit.); *shows* Q, Lucas (show Dyce,
     Hazlitt)

257 *Upon your honour?* As any quarrel that Contarino would have with Ercole
     or Romelio would be based on the injury to his honour caused by the
     contract between Jolenta and Ercole, the form of oath she requires
     here is particularly pointed.
262–3 *entangle . . . like spiders* cf. *The White Devil*, I, ii, 186–7 where the
     image of entangling is applied to silkworms. The source is Montaigne,
     III, xiii: 'Men misacknowledge the naturall infirmitie of their minde.
     She doth but quest and firret, and vncessantly goeth turning, winding,
     building and entangling her selfe in hir owne worke; as doe our silke-
     wormes, and therein stiffleth hir self'. Dent (p. 85) comments that the
     image, with Montaigne's application, became popular.

Actus Secundus, Scena Prima

Enter CRISPIANO [*disguised*], SANITONELLA

CRISPIANO

Am I well habited?

SANITONELLA

Exceeding well; any man would take you for a merchant:
but pray sir resolve me, what should be the reason, that you,
being one of the most eminent civil lawyers in Spain, and but
newly arrived from the East Indies, should take this habit   5
of a merchant upon you?

CRISPIANO

Why, my son lives here in Naples, and in's riot
Doth far exceed the exhibition I allowed him.

SANITONELLA

So then, and in this disguise you mean to trace him?

CRISPIANO

Partly for that, but there is other business   10
Of greater consequence.

SANITONELLA

Faith, for his expense, 'tis nothing to your estate. What, to
Don Crispiano, the famous corregidor of Seville, who by his
mere practice at the law, in less time than half a jubilee, hath
gotten thirty thousand ducats a year.   15

CRISPIANO

Well, I will give him line, let him

1 *habited* dressed   3 *resolve* answer
7 *riot* riotous or extravagant way of life
8 *exhibition* living allowance
12 *to* compared to
13 *corregidor* properly, the chief magistrate of a Spanish town, the
   word is here used to mean advocate; *of Seville* from Seville
   (Crispiano has been in the East Indies for 42 years)
16 *give him line* i.e., play him like a fish

This scene takes place in a street or public place and was probably acted
on the outer stage.
14 *less time . . . jubilee* Since the institution of the year of Jubilee in 1300
   by Pope Boniface VIII as a time when plenary indulgence could be
   obtained by certain acts of piety, the period between recurrences of the
   year had been reduced from a hundred years to 50 and, in 1450, to 25
   years. Nevertheless, the period of jubilee was generally thought of as
   50 years, and so Don Crispiano's success has taken less than 25 years.
   Cf. *The White Devil*, I. ii, 94.

Run on in's course of spending.
SANITONELLA   Freely?
CRISPIANO   Freely:
  For I protest, if that I could conceive
  My son would take more pleasure or content,
  By any course of riot, in the expense,   20
  Than I took joy, – nay, soul's felicity –
  In the getting of it, should all the wealth I have
  Waste to as small an atomy as flies
  I'th' sun, I do protest on that condition
  It should not move me.   25
SANITONELLA
  How's this? Cannot he take more pleasure in spending it
  riotously, than you have done by scraping it together? Oh
  ten thousand times more, and I make no question, five
  hundred young gallants will be of my opinion.
  Why, all the time of your collectionship   30
  Has been a perpetual calendar: begin first
  With your melancholy study of the law
  Before you came to finger the ruddocks; after that
  The tiring importunity of clients,
  To rise so early, and sit up so late,   35
  You made yourself half ready in a dream,
  And never prayed but in your sleep. Can I think,
  That you have half your lungs left with crying out
  For judgements, and days of trial. Remember sir,
  How often have I borne you on my shoulder,   40
  Among a shoal or swarm of reeking night-caps,
  When that your worship has bepissed yourself,
  Either with vehemency of argument,
  Or being out from the matter. I am merry.

20 *expense* spending
23 *atomy* piece as small as a mote of dust: cf. *The White Devil*, IV. ii,
    41
30 *the time of your collectionship* the time of amassing your wealth
31 *perpetual calendar* a calendar of Saints' Days, with an entry for
    every day
33 *came* ed. (come Q); *ruddocks* robin redbreasts: hence a slang term
    for gold coins
36 *ready* i.e., dressed
41 *night-caps* lawyers: cf. *The Duchess of Malfi*, II. i, 5, 22 and nn
44 *out from the matter* 'off the point, having lost your thread' (Lucas)

CRISPIANO
  Be so.   45
SANITONELLA
  You could not eat like a gentleman, at leisure;
  But swallowed it like flap-dragons, as if you had lived
  With chewing the cud after.
CRISPIANO
  No pleasure in the world was comparable to't.
SANITONELLA
  Possible?
CRISPIANO He shall never taste the like,   50
  Unless he study law.
SANITONELLA   What, not in wenching sir?
  'Tis a court game, believe it, as familiar
  As gleek, or any other.
CRISPIANO
  Wenching? Oh fie, the disease follows it:
  Beside, can the fing'ring taffaties, or lawns,   55
  Or a painted hand, or a breast, be like the pleasure
  In taking clients' fees, and piling them
  In several goodly rows before my desk?
  And according to the bigness of each heap,
  Which I took by a leer – for lawyers do not tell them –   60
  I vailed my cap, and withal gave great hope
  The cause should go on their sides.
SANITONELLA   What think you then

46 *could not* Hazlitt, Lucas (could Q, Dyce)
47 *swallowed* ed. (swallow Q); *flap-dragons* small burning objects,
    such as raisins, put into drink which had consequently to be
    swallowed very quickly
53 *gleek*, Qb (Gleeke, Qb; Gleeke Qa) (i) a three-handed card game;
    (ii) a coquettish glance. To give a person a/the gleek meant to play
    a trick upon him
55 *taffaties, or lawns* silks and fine linens used for ladies' clothes
56 *painted* artificial; decorated or adorned
60 *by a leer* by a side glance, i.e., not seeming interested in the fees;
    tell count
61 *vailed* took off as a sign of respect and acknowledgement of
    inferiority

54 ff. As Lucas pointed out (II, 331), Crispiano's sentiments here con-
    flict with his character as revealed later in the play.

Of a good cry of hounds? It has been known
Dogs have hunted lordships to a fault.
CRISPIANO   Cry of curs?
The noise of clients at my chamber door   65
Was sweeter music far, in my conceit,
Than all the hunting in Europe.
SANITONELLA   Pray stay sir,
Say he should spend it in good housekeeping.
CRISPIANO
Ay marry sir, to have him keep a good house,
And not sell't away, I'd find no fault with that: 70
But his kitchen, I'd have no bigger than a saw-pit;
For the smallness of a kitchen, without question,
Makes many noblemen in France and Spain
Build the rest of the house the bigger.
SANITONELLA   Yes, mock-beggars.
CRISPIANO
Some sevenscore chimneys, but half of them   75
Have no tunnels.
SANITONELLA   A pox upon them! Kickshaws,
That beget such monsters without fundaments.
CRISPIANO
Come, come, leave citing other vanities;
For neither wine, nor lust, nor riotous feasts,
Rich clothes, nor all the pleasure that the devil   80
Has ever practised with, to raise a man
To a devil's likeness, e'er brought man that pleasure
I took in getting my wealth: so I conclude.

63–4 *cry* pack; barking
66 *conceit* opinion
71 *saw-pit* a small pit over which a frame was erected for sawing
   timber
74 *mock-beggars*: 'with a pun on "bigger". This word was regularly
   applied to fine, but inhospitable houses' (Lucas)
76 *Kickshaws* from French *quelques choses;* originally applied to
   light and frivolous culinary dishes, the word by transference came
   to mean light and frivolous people
77 *fundaments* anuses

---

64 *Dogs . . . fault* Dogs have hunted down estates until checked by a
   failure of the scent, i.e., the expense of hunting has continued until a
   gentleman has been financially ruined.
71–4 The idea of a small kitchen making a large house was proverbial: see
   Tilley, K 111.

If he can out-vie me, let it fly to th'devil.
Yon's my son; what company keeps he?

Enter ROM[ELIO], JULIO, ARIOSTO, BAPTISTA

SANITONELLA   The gentleman   85
He talks with, is Romelio the merchant.
CRISPIANO
I never saw him till now;
'A has a brave sprightly look; I knew his father,
And sojourned in his house two years together,
Before this young man's birth. I have news to tell him   90
Of certain losses happened him at sea,
That will not please him.
SANITONELLA   What's that dapper fellow
In the long stocking? I do think 'twas he
Came to your lodging this morning.
CRISPIANO   'Tis the same.
There he stands, but a little piece of flesh,   95
But he is the very miracle of a lawyer,
One that persuades men to peace, and compounds quarrels
Among his neighbours, without going to law.
SANITONELLA
And is he a lawyer?
CRISPIANO   Yes, and will give counsel
In honest causes gratis; never in his life   100
Took fee, but he came and spake for't; is a man
Of extreme practice, and yet all his longing,
Is to become a judge.
SANITONELLA
Indeed that's a rare longing with men of his profession.
I think he'll prove the miracle of a lawyer indeed.   105
ROMELIO
Here's the man brought word your father died i'th' Indies.
JULIO
He died in perfect memory I hope,
And made me his heir.
CRISPIANO   Yes sir.
JULIO
He's gone the right way, then, without question. Friend, in

92 *What's* ed. (What Q)
97 *compounds* settles
102 *extreme practice* strict or stringent habit
107 *in perfect memory* in sound mind and consequently capable of
     making a will that would stand in law

time of mourning, we must not use any action, that is but 110
accessory to the making men merry; I do therefore give you
nothing for your good tidings.

CRISPIANO
Nor do I look for it sir.

JULIO
Honest fellow, give me thy hand. I do not think but thou
hast carried New-Year's-gifts to th' court in thy days, and 115
learn'd'st there to be so free of thy pains-taking.

ROMELIO
Here's an old gentleman says he was chamber-fellow to your
father, when they studied the law together at Barcelona.

JULIO
Do you know him?

ROMELIO
Not I, he's newly come to Naples. 120

JULIO
And what's his business?

ROMELIO
'A says he's come to read you good counsel.

CRISPIANO *This is spoke aside [to* ARIOSTO]
To him, rate him soundly.

JULIO
And what's your counsel?

ARIOSTO
Why, I would have you leave your whoring. 125

JULIO
He comes hotly upon me at first: whoring?

ARIOSTO
Oh young quat, incontinence is plagued
In all the creatures of the world!

JULIO
When did you ever hear, that a cocksparrow
Had the French pox? 130

ARIOSTO
When did you ever know any of them fat, but in the nest?

123 s.d.: opposite l. 123 in Q; *rate* berate, scold
127 *quat* pimple; hence a contemptuous term for a young person
128 *world!* Dyce, Hazlitt (world. Q, Lucas)

129–30 Lucas suggested a source in Overbury's *Characters*, 'Newes from
the very Countrie', signed I.D. and attributed to John Donne (Lucas,
II, 332).

Ask all your cantharide-mongers that question; remember
yourself sir.

JULIO
A very fine naturalist! A physician, I take you by your round
slop; for 'tis just of the bigness, and no more, of the case for a   135
urinal: 'tis concluded, you are a physician. [ARIOSTO *removes
his hat*] What do you mean sir? You'll take cold.

ARIOSTO
'Tis concluded, you are a fool, a precious one: you are a
mere stick of sugar candy; a man may look quite thorough
you.   140

JULIO
You are a very bold gamester. [JULIO *removes his hat*]

ARIOSTO
I can play at chess, and know how to handle a rook.

JULIO
Pray preserve your velvet from the dust.

ARIOSTO
Keep you hat upon the block sir, 'twill continue fashion the
longer.   145

JULIO
I was never so abused with the hat in the hand
In my life.

ARIOSTO   I will put on. [*He replaces his hat*] Why look you,
Those lands that were the client's are now become
The lawyer's; and those tenements that were
The country gentleman's are now grown   150
To be his tailor's.

---

132 *cantharide-mongers* i.e., apothecaries; cantharides, made from
    Spanish fly (*cantharis vesicatoria*) was a poison which, taken in
    small quantities, was considered to have both medicinal and
    aphrodisiac properties: see *The White Devil*, II. i, 284 and nn;
    Lucas, II, 332
135 *slop* wide breeches
142 *rook* (i) castle in chess; (ii) gull or simpleton
144 *block* wooden moulding block to keep hats in shape; Julio's
    (wooden) head; *continue fashion* stay fashionable, i.e., in good shape

---

138–40 repeated verbatim from *The Duchess of Malfi*, III. i, 42–3, where the
    Duchess comments on Ferdinand's suggestion that she marry Count
    Malateste:
        . . . He's a mere stick of sugar-candy,
        You may look quite thorough him: . . .
148–51 from Jonson, *The Devil is an Ass*, II. iv, 33–7.

JULIO
  Tailor's?
ARIOSTO
  Yes, tailors in France, they grow to great abominable
  purchase, and become great officers. How many ducats
  think you he has spent within a twelvemonth, besides his   155
  father's allowance?
JULIO
  Besides my father's allowance? Why gentleman, do you
  think an auditor begat me? Would you have me make even at
  year's end?
ROMELIO
  A hundred ducats a month in breaking Venice glasses.   160
ARIOSTO
  He learnt that of an English drunkard, and a knight too,
  as I take it. This comes of your numerous wardrobe.
ROMELIO
  Ay, and wearing cut-work, a pound a purl.
ARIOSTO
  Your dainty embroidered stockings, with overblown roses, to
  hide your gouty ankles.   165
ROMELIO
  And wearing more taffaty for a garter, than would serve the
  galley dung-boat for streamers.
ARIOSTO
  Your switching up at the horse-race, with the illustrissimi.

154 *purchase* substance, acquired wealth: cf. *The Duchess of Malfi*, III.
     i, 28
162 *numerous* copious; comprising many different items
163 *cut-work* see I. ii, 162n: *purl* pleat or fold of a ruff or band, par-
     ticularly fashionable in the beginning of the 17th century
164 *roses* large knots or rosettes of ribbon: cf. *The White Devil*, V. iii,
     103
166 *taffaty* Q, Lucas (taffeta Dyce; taffata Hazlitt) fine, shiny silk: cf.
     II. i, 55n
167 *galley dung-boat for streamers* on a festive occasion the large row-
     ing-boat, normally used for carrying manure, would be decorated
     with ribbons
168 *switching up* riding about; *illustrissimi* best society; 'nobs'

162 ff. Dent indicates further borrowing from *The Devil is an Ass* here: cf.
     The Devil is an Ass, I. i, 126–30 and III. iii, 22–30. He also points out
     that Ariosto's sudden mention of food in ll. 173–4 is accounted for by
     the source in the second passage (Dent, pp. 297–8).

ROMELIO
And studying a puzzling arithmetic at the cock-pit.
ARIOSTO
Shaking your elbow at the taule-board.   170
ROMELIO
And resorting to your whore in hired velvet, with a spangled
copper fringe at her netherlands.
ARIOSTO
Whereas if you had stayed at Padua, and fed upon cow-
trotters, and fresh beef to supper –
JULIO
How I am baited!   175
ARIOSTO
Nay, be not you so forward with him neither, for 'tis thought
you'll prove a main part of his undoing.
JULIO
I think this fellow is a witch –
ROMELIO
Who, I sir?
ARIOSTO
You have certain rich city chuffs, that when they have no   180
acres of their own, they will go and plough up fools, and turn
them into excellent meadow; besides some enclosures for the
first cherries in the spring, and apricocks to pleasure a friend

169 *puzzling . . . cock-pit* complicated betting on the results of cock-
fights
170 *taule-board* table-board: 'Tables (Lat. *Tabularum lusus*, Fr.
Tables,) is the old name for backgammon: but other games were
played with the same board' (Dyce)
171 *hired velvet* worn by the whore, not by Julio
171–2 *spangled copper fringe* 'imitating gold lace. So we hear of
gallants at the theatre betting whether the actors' gold lace is real
or gilt' (Lucas)
172 *netherlands*: 'backside; with a quibble upon the numerous Dutch
whores in London' (Gunby)
173–4 *if . . . supper* – if you had stayed at the university and dined on
the usual student fare
178 *witch* – ed. (witch Q; witch. Dyce, Hazlitt, Lucas)
180 *chuffs* boors; misers
182 *meadow* pasture
182–4 i.e., the poor gallants are gulled into providing delicacies for
the chuffs

180–2 from Jonson, *The Devil is an Ass*, III. iv, 45–8.

at court with. You have pothecaries deal in selling commodi-
ties to young gallants, will put four or five coxcombs into a   185
sieve, and so drum with them upon their counter; they'll
searce them through like Guinea pepper: they cannot endure
to find a man like a pair of tarriers, they would undo him in a
trice.

ROMELIO
May be there are such.   190

ARIOSTO
Oh terrible exactors, fellows with six hands, and three heads.

JULIO
Ay, those are hell-hounds.

ARIOSTO
Take heed of them, they'll rent thee like tenterhooks. Hark
in your ear, there is intelligence upon you; the report goes,
there has been gold conveyed beyond the sea in hollow   195

---

186 *counter* (i) shop-counter; (ii) the Counter, the debtors' prison in
     London
187 *searce* sieve
191–2 in classical mythology Hell was guarded by the three-headed
     dog, Cerberus
193 *tenterhooks* nails used to stretch newly-woven cloth on the tenter,
     or wooden framework, to prevent it from shrinking
194 *there is intelligence upon you* information has been laid about you.
     (An intelligencer was a spy.)

184–5 *selling . . . gallants* This trick of lending foolish young gentlemen
     goods instead of cash and then demanding repayment in cash at an
     inflated estimate of their value is one of the notorious offences whose
     perpetrators' names are recorded in Monticelso's black book: see *The
     White Devil*, IV. i, 50–1.
187 *Guinea pepper Piper clussi*, DC., was known in Europe as early as 1364,
     but in 1485 King John II of Portugal prevented its importation into
     Europe in case the value of Indian pepper depreciated. In the 16th
     century English traders voyaged to the Guinea Coast for gold, ivory,
     Guinea pepper, and another speciality of the region, Guinea grains—
     the seeds of *Aframonum melegueta*—also known as grains of paradise.
188 *a pair of tarriers* Tarriers, tiring irons, is a puzzle of great antiquity,
     in which 7 or 10 rings are placed on an oblong closed wire loop or bow,
     each ring being also fastened to a wire within the loop, which passes
     through the next ring, and is loosely attached by its other end to a thin
     flat piece of metal or bone of nearly the same length as the loop. The
     puzzle consists in discovering how to take all the rings thus fettered off
     the loop.

anchors. Farewell, you shall know me better, I will do
thee more good, than thou art aware of.

Exit AR[IOSTO]

JULIO

He's a mad fellow.

SANITONELLA

He would have made an excellent barber, he does so curry it
with his tongue.   *Exit*   200

CRISPIANO

Sir, I was directed to you.

ROMELIO

From whence?

CRISPIANO

From the East Indies.

ROMELIO

You are very welcome.

CRISPIANO

Please you walk apart,   205
I shall acquaint you with particulars
Touching your trading i'th' East Indies.

ROMELIO

Willingly; pray walk sir.   *Ex[eunt]* CRIS[PIANO,] ROM[ELIO]

Enter ERCOLE

ERCOLE

Oh my right worthy friends, you have stayed me long;
One health, and then aboard; for all the galleys   210
Are come about.

Enter CONTARINO

---

197 s.d.: opposite l. 198 in Q
199 *curry* use as a comb; scratch
209 *stayed* waited for
210–11 *the galleys/Are come about* the galleys have returned to port:
    cf. *The Duchess of Malfi*, I. ii, 71

195–6 *gold conveyed . . . anchors* Sending gold or coin abroad was a serious
    offence in the Middle Ages and statutes for its prohibition were issued
    from the reigns of Henry VI to Henry VIII. In 1618 it was discovered
    that £7 million had been smuggled out of England by foreign mer-
    chants, mainly Dutch, in the previous 15 years, and the following
    summer the case was tried in the Court of Star Chamber, causing con-
    siderable excitement. See Lucas I, 254 and II, 334. In his dying agonies
    Brachiano accuses Flamineo of having conveyed coin out of his terri-
    tories: *The White Devil*, V. iii, 83.

CONTARINO   Signior Ercole,
  The wind has stood my friend sir, to prevent
  Your putting to sea.
ERCOLE   Pray why sir?
CONTARINO   Only love sir,
  That I might take my leave sir, and withal
  Entreat from you a private recommends   215
  To a friend in Malta; 'twould be delivered
  To your bosom, for I had no time to write.
ERCOLE
  Pray leave us gentlemen.   *Exeunt* [JULIO *and* BAPTISTA]
                Wilt please you sit?
                        They sit down
CONTARINO
  Sir, my love to you has proclaimed you one,
  Whose word was still led by a noble thought,   220
  And that thought followed by as fair a deed.
  Deceive not that opinion; we were students
  At Padua together, and have long
  To th' world's eye shown like friends.
  Was it hearty on your part to me?
ERCOLE   Unfeigned.
CONTARINO   You are false   225
  To the good thought I held of you, and now
  Join the worst part of man to you, your malice,
  To uphold that falsehood; sacred innocence
  Is fled your bosom. Signior, I must tell you,
  To draw the picture of unkindness truly,   230
  Is to express two that have dearly loved,
  And fall'n at variance; 'tis a wonder to me,
  Knowing my interest in the fair Jolenta
  That you should love her.

215 *recommends* recommendation
220 *still* constantly; invariably
225 *hearty* sincere

219ff. Of his choice of this scene for inclusion in his *Specimens of English Dramatic Poets, who lived about the time of Shakespeare: with notes* (1808) Charles Lamb wrote, 'I have selected this scene as the model of a well-managed and gentlemanlike difference' (p. 199n).
220–1 cf. *Arcadia*, I, v, of Argalus: 'his worde ever ledde by his thought, and followed by his deede' (Dent, p. 299).

ERCOLE

Compare her beauty and my youth together,   235
And you will find the fair effects of love
No miracle at all.

CONTARINO   Yes, it will prove
Prodigious to you. I must stay your voyage.

ERCOLE

Your warrant must be mighty.

CONTARINO   'T has a seal
From heaven to do it, since you would ravish from me   240
What's there entitled mine: and yet I vow,
By the essential front of spotless virtue,
I have compassion of both our youths:
To approve which, I have not ta'en the way,
Like an Italian, to cut your throat   245
By practice, that had given you now for dead,
And never frowned upon you.

ERCOLE   You deal fair, sir.

CONTARINO

Quit me of one doubt, pray sir.

ERCOLE   Move it.

CONTARINO   'Tis this,
Whether her brother were a main instrument
In her design for marriage.   250

ERCOLE   If I tell truth,
You will not credit me.

CONTARINO   Why?

ERCOLE   I will tell you truth,
Yet show some reason you have not to believe me.
Her brother had no hand in't; — is't not hard
For you to credit this? — for you may think

238 *Prodigious* ominous; *stay* prevent
239 *'T has* ed.: see Textual Appendix A
242 *essential* real, actual
246 *By practice* by treachery, in an underhand way
248 *Quit* rid; *Move* mention

235–7 Dent points out that these lines are closer to their source in *Arcadia*,
    V—'Let her beawtie be compared to my yeares, and such effectes will
    be found no miracles'—than the parallel passage in *The Duchess of
    Malfi*, V. ii, 163–4, where Julia tells Bosola:
            Compare thy form and my eyes together,
            You'll find my love no such great miracle.
                                            (Dent, p. 299)

I count it baseness to engage another   255
Into my quarrel; and for that take leave
To dissemble the truth. Sir, if you will fight
With any but myself, fight with her mother;
She was the motive.

CONTARINO
I have no enemy in the world then, but yourself;   260
You must fight with me.

ERCOLE   I will sir.

CONTARINO   And instantly.

ERCOLE
I will haste before you; point whither.

CONTARINO
Why, you speak nobly, and for this fair dealing,
Were the rich jewel which we vary for,
A thing to be divided, by my life,   265
I would be well content to give you half:
But since 'tis vain to think we can be friends,
'Tis needful one of us be ta'en away,
From being the other's enemy.

ERCOLE   Yet methinks,
This looks not like a quarrel.

CONTARINO   Not a quarrel?   270

ERCOLE
You have not apparelled your fury well,
It goes too plain, like a scholar.

CONTARINO   It is an ornament
Makes it more terrible, and you shall find it
A weighty injury, and attended on
By discreet valour; because I do not strike you,   275

---

259 *motive* instigator   264 *vary* fall at variance, quarrel

272 *like a scholar* University scholars were ordered to dress soberly at this time—which is why Dr Faustus, intoxicated with the dreams of diabolic power, promises to 'fill the public schools with silk/Wherewith the students shall be bravely clad'.

275–6 *because ... preparatives* Striking or giving a man the lie was a formal method of leading up to a duel and Elizabethan and Jacobean gentlemen were very punctilious in the observation of the rules of quarrelling. The theory of the honourable quarrel, seriously expounded in such works as *Vincentio Saviolo his practise* (1594; 1595) and Sir William Segar's *The Booke of Honor and Armes* (1590) and *Honor, Military and Ciuill* (1602), was mocked by Touchstone in *As You Like It*, V. iv, 48–97.

Or give you the lie, such foul preparatives
Would show like the stale injury of wine.
I reserve my rage to sit on my sword's point,
Which a great quantity of your best blood
Cannot satisfy.
ERCOLE   You promise well to yourself.   280
Shall's have no seconds?
CONTARINO   None, for fear of prevention.
ERCOLE
The length of our weapons?
CONTARINO   We'll fit them by the way:
So whether our time calls us to live or die,
Let us do both like noble gentlemen,
And true Italians.
ERCOLE   For that let me embrace you.   285
                                  [*They embrace*]
CONTARINO
Methinks, being an Italian, I trust you
To come somewhat too near me:
But your jealousy gave that embrace to try
If I were armed, did it not?
ERCOLE   No, believe me,
I take your heart to be sufficient proof,   290
Without a privy coat; and for my part,
A taffaty is all the shirt of mail
I am armed with.
CONTARINO   You deal equally.   *Exeunt*

                  Enter JULIO, *and* SERVANT

JULIO
Where are these gallants, the brave Ercole,

290 *proof* (i) evidence; (ii) firmness that resists impression and does not
       yield to force
291 *privy coat* a coat of mail worn for defence, secretly, as it was
       against the law of duelling to wear one
292 *taffaty* i.e., a thin silk doublet
293 *equally* justly

283–5: another borrowing from *Arcadia* (I, iv), which Webster had also
       used in *The Duchess of Malfi* (III. ii, 70–1). This time too, *The Devil's
       Law-Case* is closer to the source: 'Lastly, whether your time call you to
       live or die, doo both like a prince' (Dent, pp. 209, 299).
286 *being an Italian* an allusion to the secretly vindictive character which
       Jacobean Englishmen attributed to Italians.

And noble Contarino?

SERVANT   They are newly gone sir,   295
And bade me tell you, that they will return
Within this half hour.

Enter ROMELIO

JULIO   Met you the Lord Ercole?
ROMELIO
No, but I met the devil in villainous tidings.
JULIO
Why, what's the matter?
ROMELIO   Oh I am poured out
Like water; the greatest rivers i'th' world   300
Are lost in the sea, and so am I: pray leave me.
Where's Lord Ercole?
JULIO   You were scarce gone hence,
But in came Contarino.
ROMELIO   Contarino?
JULIO
And entreated some private conference with Ercole,
And on the sudden they have given's the slip.   305
ROMELIO
One mischief never comes alone:
They are gone to fight.
JULIO   To fight?
ROMELIO   And you be gentlemen,
Do not talk, but make haste after them.
JULIO
Let's take several ways then,
And if't be possible, for women's sakes,   310
For they are proper men, use our endeavours,
That the prick do not spoil them.

                          Exeunt

298 *in villainous tidings* in the form of villainous tidings
307 *And you* if you
309 *several* different
311 *proper* handsome
312 *prick* wounding, i.e., duelling; *spoil* disfigure

300–1 As Dent indicates (p. 299), Webster's ultimate source is Ecclesiastes,
    i, 7: 'All the rivers run into the sea; yet the sea is not full; . . .'

[Act II, Scene ii]

Enter ERCOLE, CONTARINO

CONTARINO
    You'll not forgo your interest in my mistress?
ERCOLE
    My sword shall answer that; come, are you ready?
CONTARINO
    Before you fight sir, think upon your cause;
    It is a wondrous foul one, and I wish,
    That all your exercise these four days past,   5
    Had been employed in a most fervent prayer,
    And the foul sin for which you are to fight
    Chiefly remembered in't.
ERCOLE   I'd as soon take
    Your counsel in divinity at this present
    As I would take a kind direction from you   10
    For the managing my weapon; and indeed,
    Both would show much alike.
    Come, are you ready?
CONTARINO   Bethink yourself,
    How fair the object is that we contend for.
ERCOLE
    Oh, I cannot forget it.   *They fight*
CONTARINO   You are hurt.   15
ERCOLE
    Did you come hither only to tell me so,
    Or to do it? I mean well, but 'twill not thrive.
CONTARINO
    Your cause, your cause sir:
    Will you yet be a man of conscience, and make
    Restitution for your rage upon your death-bed?   20
ERCOLE
    Never, till the grave gather one of us.
             Fight [CONTARINO *wounds* ERCOLE]
CONTARINO
    That was fair, and home I think.

---

17 *I . . . thrive* I mean to fight well, but the duel goes against me

---

This scene takes place in a field, and is presented on the outer stage.
Lucas (II, 335) indicates a very striking resemblance between this
duel and one described by Edward Sackville in 1613 and printed by
Steele in *The Guardian*, No. 133 (13 August 1713).

ERCOLE
   You prate as if you were in a fence-school.
CONTARINO
   Spare your youth, have compassion on yourself.
ERCOLE
   When I am all in pieces! I am now unfit   25
   For any lady's bed; take the rest with you.
                     CONTARINO *wounded, falls upon* ERCOLE
CONTARINO
   I am lost in too much daring: yield your sword.
ERCOLE
   To the pangs of death I shall, but not to thee.
CONTARINO
   You are now at my repairing, or confusion:
   Beg your life.
ERCOLE   Oh most foolishly demanded,   30
   To bid me beg that which thou canst not give.

Enter ROMELIO, PROSP[ERO,] BAPT[ISTA,] ARIO[STO,] JULIO

PROSPERO
   See, both of them are lost; we come too late.
ROMELIO
   Take up the body, and convey it
   To Saint Sebastian's monastery.
CONTARINO
   I will not part with his sword, I have won't.
JULIO   You shall not.   35
   Take him up gently: so, and bow his body,
   For fear of bleeding inward.
   Well, these are perfect lovers.
PROSPERO   Why, I pray?
JULIO
   It has been ever my opinion,
   That there are none love perfectly indeed,   40
   But those that hang or drown themselves for love:
   Now these have chose a death next to beheading,
   They have cut one another's throats, brave valiant lads.
PROSPERO
   Come, you do ill, to set the name of valour
   Upon a violent and mad despair.   45
   Hence may all learn, that count such actions well,
   The roots of fury shoot themselves to hell.   *Exeunt*

29–30 i.e., you are now at my mercy, to save or kill you
35 *won't* won it

[Act II, Scene iii]

Enter ROMELIO, ARIOSTO

ARIOSTO
    Your losses, I confess, are infinite,
    Yet sir, you must have patience.
ROMELIO   Sir, my losses
    I know, but you I do not.
ARIOSTO   'Tis most true,
    I am but a stranger to you, but am wished,
    By some of your best friends, to visit you,   5
    And out of my experience in the world,
    To instruct you patience.
ROMELIO   Of what profession are you?
ARIOSTO
    Sir, I am a lawyer.
ROMELIO   Of all men living,
    You lawyers I account the only men
    To confirm patience in us; your delays   10
    Would make three parts of this little Christian world
    Run out of their wits else. Now I remember,
    You read lectures to Julio. Are you such a leech
    For patience?
ARIOSTO   Yes sir, I have had some crosses.
ROMELIO
    You are married then, I am certain.
ARIOSTO   That I am sir.   15
ROMELIO
    And have you studied patience?
ARIOSTO   You shall find I have.
ROMELIO
    Did you ever see your wife make you cuckold?
ARIOSTO
    Make me cuckold?
ROMELIO
    I ask it seriously: and you have not seen that,
    Your patience has not ta'en the right degree   20
    Of wearing scarlet; I should rather take you

13 *leech* physician
21 *scarlet* i.e., the scarlet robes of a doctor's degree

This scene is set in Leonora's house and occupies the whole stage, the
outer stage representing the courtyard: see Lucas, II, 335.

For a Bachelor in the Art, than for a Doctor.

ARIOSTO
You are merry.

ROMELIO   No sir, with leave of your patience,
I am horrible angry.

ARIOSTO   What should move you
Put forth that harsh interrogatory, if these eyes   25
Ever saw my wife do the thing you wot of?

ROMELIO
Why, I'll tell you:
Most radically to try your patience,
And the mere question shows you but a dunce in't.
It has made you angry; there's another lawyer's beard   30
In your forehead, you do bristle.

ARIOSTO
You are very conceited.
But come, this is not the right way to cure you.
I must talk to you like a divine.

ROMELIO   I have heard
Some talk of it very much, and many times   35
To their auditors' impatience; but I pray,
What practice do they make of't in their lives?
They are too full of choler with living honest,
And some of them not only impatient
Of their own slightest injuries, but stark mad,   40
At one another's preferment: now to you sir,
I have lost three goodly carracks.

ARIOSTO   So I hear.

ROMELIO
The very spice in them,
Had they been shipwracked here upon our coast,
Would have made all our sea a drench.   45

ARIOSTO
All the sick horses in Italy

---

25 *interrogatory* in law, a question formally put to a witness
32 *conceited* full of conceits or jests
41 *preferment* promotion
42 *carracks* large cargo vessels
45 *drench* a dose of medicine, especially for an animal, including such
   ingredients as myrrh, oil of spikenard, and pepper

34–6 Like its parallel in *The White Devil*, V. vi, 65–70, this passage has a
   source in Montaigne, III, 4: 'Even as Preachers exclamations do often
   move their auditory more then their reasons' (Lucas, I, 265).

Would have been glad of your loss then.
ROMELIO
You are conceited too.
ARIOSTO   Come, come, come,
You gave those ships most strange, most dreadful,
And unfortunate names, I never looked they'd prosper.   50
ROMELIO
Is there any ill omen in giving names to ships?
ARIOSTO
Did you not call one, *The Storm's Defiance*;
Another, *The Scourge of the Sea*; and the third, *The Great
Leviathan*?
ROMELIO   Very right sir.
ARIOSTO   Very devilish names
All three of them: and surely I think they were cursed   55
In their very cradles; I do mean, when they
Were upon their stocks.
ROMELIO   Come, you are superstitious;
I'll give you my opinion, and 'tis serious:
I am persuaded there came not cuckolds enow
To the first launching of them, and 'twas that   60
Made them thrive the worse for't. Oh your cuckold's handsel
Is prayed for i'th' city.
ARIOSTO   I will hear no more,
Give me thy hand: my intent of coming hither,
Was to persuade you to patience; as I live,

57 *stocks* framework which supports a ship under construction
59 *enow* enough
61 *handsel* first use of a thing; Lucas says that 'Cuckold's luck was
    proverbially good'

49–57 Elizabethan and Jacobean sailors were convinced that a charm lay
in the name of their ship. For this reason 'Bonadventure' was popular.
In the poem *The Trumpet of Fame* (1595) which celebrates the achieve-
ments of Drake and Hawkins, the ships which made the descent on
Puerto Rico are seen to have been significantly named 'Garland', 'Hope',
'Foresight', 'Concord', and 'Amity'. In his *Voyage into the South Sea*
(1622) Sir Richard Hawkins gave examples of vessels whose badly
chosen names, such as 'The Revenge' and 'Thunderbolt', brought
them ill fortune. Hawkins's own ship, 'The Repentance', had bad luck,
and in William Kidley's poem *Hawkins* (1624) the hero is represented
as protesting against this choice of name, made by his mother. See R. R.
Cawley, *Unpathed Waters: Studies in the Influence of the Voyagers on
Elizabethan Literature* (Princeton, 1940), pp. 150–1, 201–2 and Lucas,
II, 335–6.

If ever I do visit you again, 65
It shall be to entreat you to be angry, sure I will,
I'll be as good as my word, believe it. *Exit*

Enter LEONORA

ROMELIO
So sir. How now?
Are the screech-owls abroad already?

LEONORA
What a dismal noise yon bell makes; 70
Sure some great person's dead.

ROMELIO No such matter;
It is the common bellman goes about,
To publish the sale of goods.

LEONORA Why do they ring
Before my gate thus? Let them into th'court,
I cannot understand what they say. 75

Enter two BELLMEN *and a* CAPUCHIN

CAPUCHIN
For pity's sake, you that have tears to shed,
Sigh a soft requiem, and let fall a bead,
For two unfortunate nobles, whose sad fate
Leaves them both dead, and excommunicate:
No churchman's prayer to comfort their last groans, 80
No sacred seed of earth to hide their bones;
But as their fury wrought them out of breath,

---

67 s.d.: opposite l.63 in Q
75 s.d. CAPUCHIN: opposite l. 75 in Q
77 *bead* prayer; each bead of a rosary represents a prayer
81 *seed* Q (sod Dyce)
82 *out of breath* (i) breathless; (ii) lifeless

69ff. These lines echo *The Duchess of Malfi*, IV. ii, 170ff. both in tone and
in specific references to the bellman and the screech-owl as well as in
the use of a formal dirge.
72 *bellman* The bellman rang his bell to attract attention for announce-
ments of deaths and requests for prayers for the dead. In 1605 Robert
Dowe of the Merchant Taylors' Company gave an endowment to pay
the clerk of St Sepulchre's to toll the bell and go himself as bellman to
exhort condemned prisoners in Newgate the night before their execution. Webster was born free of the Merchant Taylors' Company and his
name is among the signatures to Dowe's endowment. Dowe died in
1612. Cf. *The Duchess of Malfi*, IV. ii, 170–1.
75 s.d.: CAPUCHIN: see above, p. 3.

The canon speaks them guilty of their own death.

LEONORA

What noblemen, I pray sir?

CAPUCHIN   The Lord Ercole,
And the noble Contarino, both of them   85
Slain in single combat.

LEONORA   Oh, I am lost for ever!

ROMELIO

Denied Christian burial – I pray what does that,
Or the dead lazy march in the funeral
Or the flattery in the epitaphs, which shows
More sluttish far than all the spiders' webs   90
Shall ever grow upon it: what do these
Add to our well-being after death?

CAPUCHIN

Not a scruple.

ROMELIO   Very well then:
I have a certain meditation,
If I can think of't, somewhat to this purpose;   95
I'll say it to you, while my mother there
Numbers her beads.

You that dwell near these graves and vaults,
Which oft do hide physicians' faults,
Note what a small room does suffice   100
To express men's good; their vanities
Would fill more volume in small hand,
Than all the evidence of church-land.
Funerals hide men in civil wearing,

83 *canon* ecclesiastical or divine decree
89 *epitaphs* i.e., on the tombstones
95 *of't* Hazlitt (of Q; of ['t] Dyce, Lucas)
102 *hand* handwriting
103 *evidence* title-deeds; *church-land* see I. i, 177n

83 i.e., 'Divine law judges them guilty of their murders'. For this reason
    they are excommunicate: cf. *Hamlet*, I. ii, 131–2.
98ff. The punctuation of Q, with every line except 111 and 112 ending in
    a comma or full stop, suggests, by its similarity to the punctuation of
    The Duchess of Malfi, IV. ii, 175–92, that Romelio may have sung, or
    at least chanted, this meditation.
98–103 cf. *Hamlet*, V. i, 104–5: 'The very conveyance of his lands will
    hardly lie in this box; and must the inheritor himself have no more,
    ha?'

And are to the drapers a good hearing,   105
Make the heralds laugh in their black raiment,
And all die worthies die worth payment.
To the altar offerings, though their fame,
And all the charity of their name,
'Tween heaven and this yield no more light   110
Than rotten trees, which shine i'th' night.
Oh look the last act be the best i'th' play,
And then rest, gentle bones; yet pray,
That when by the precise you are viewed,
A supersedeas be not sued,   115
To remove you to a place more airy,
That in your stead they may keep chary
Stockfish, or seacoal, for the abuses
Of sacrilege have turned graves to vilder uses.
How then can any monument say,   120
'Here rest these bones till the last day',
When time swift both of foot and feather
May bear them the sexton kens not whither?
What care I then, though my last sleep
Be in the desert, or in the deep,   125
No lamp, nor taper, day and night,
To give my charnel chargeable light?
I have there like quantity of ground,
And at the last day I shall be found.

   Now I pray leave me.
CAPUCHIN   I am sorry for your losses.   130

105 *a good hearing* good news
107 i.e., 'All die honoured who leave enough money to pay for their
    own funerals'
113 *rest, gentle bones;* ed. (rest gentle bones, Q)
117 *chary* charily, frugally: here used as an adverb
121 quotation marks: ed.
127 *charnel* burial vault; *chargeable* expensive

114–15 Puritans (*the precise*) would if necessary take legal action to obtain
    even a charnel-house for business purposes. A *supersedeas* is a writ
    commanding the stay of legal proceedings.
119 *vilder uses* Lucas calls attention to lines in Marston's *Sophonisba*
    (1606), IV. i, 157–60 which indicate that one of the more vile uses of
    old vaults was as a rustic privy

ROMELIO

Um sir, the more spacious that the tennis-court is,
The more large is the hazard.
I dare the spiteful Fortune do her worst,
I can now fear nothing.

CAPUCHIN   Oh sir, yet consider,
He that is without fear is without hope,   135
And sins from presumption; better thoughts attend you.

          Exit CA[PUCHIN *with* BELLMEN]

ROMELIO

Poor Jolenta! Should she hear of this,
She would not after the report keep fresh
So long as flowers in graves.

          Enter PROSPERO

          How now, Prospero?

PROSPERO

Contarino has sent you here his will,   140
Wherein 'a has made your sister his sole heir.

ROMELIO

Is he not dead?

PROSPERO   He's yet living.

ROMELIO   Living? the worse luck.

LEONORA

The worse? I do protest it is the best
That ever came to disturb my prayers.

ROMELIO   How!

LEONORA

Yet I would have him live   145
To satisfy public justice for the death

133 *Fortune* i.e., the goddess Fortune
136 *sins from presumption* sins through the pride of assuming that he
     knows more about his own fate than God does
137 *Jolenta!* Dyce, Hazlitt (*Jolenta*, Q, Lucas); *this*, Dyce, Hazlitt
     (*this?* Q; this! Lucas)
139 s.d.: opposite l. 139a in Q
141 *'a* he   142; 145 *yet* still
143 *The worse?* Lucas (The worse: Q; The worse! Dyce, Hazlitt)

131–2 *tennis-court . . . hazard* cf. *The White Devil*, V. i, 71–3. The original
     game of tennis was played indoors on a court whose two sides were called
     the service side and the hazard side. The *hazard* is one of the openings,
     of which there are two on the hazard side and one on the service side,
     on the inner wall of the court, into which a winning stroke may be played.
     Used metaphorically, *hazard* means peril or jeopardy.

Of Ercole. Oh go visit him, for heaven's sake!
I have within my closet a choice relic,
Preservative 'gainst swounding, and some earth
Brought from the Holy Land, right sovereign   150
To stanch blood: has he skilful surgeons, think you?
PROSPERO
The best in Naples!
ROMELIO   How oft has he been dressed?
PROSPERO
But once.
LEONORA   I have some skill this way:
The second or third dressing will show clearly
Whether there be hope of life. I pray be near him,   155
If there be any soul can bring me word,
That there is hope of life.
ROMELIO
Do you prize his life so?
LEONORA   That he may live, I mean,
To come to his trial, to satisfy the law.
ROMELIO
Oh, is't nothing else?
LEONORA   I shall be the happiest woman.   160
                    Exeunt LE[ONORA,] PRO[SPERO]
ROMELIO
Here is cruelty apparelled in kindness.
I am full of thoughts, strange ones, but they're no good ones.
I must visit Contarino, upon that
Depends an engine shall weigh up my losses,
Were they sunk as low as hell; yet let me think   165
How I am impaired in an hour, and the cause of't,
Lost in security. Oh how this wicked world bewitches,
Especially made insolent with riches!
So sails with fore-winds stretched do soonest break,
And pyramids a'th' top are still most weak.   170
                    Exit

149 *swounding* swooning
150 *sovereign* efficacious
159 *satisfy the law* i.e., to answer for the murder of Ercole
164 *engine* device, plot; *weigh up* raise, as the lightened side of a
     balance rises upwards; counterpoise
167 *security* freedom from anxiety; carelessness: for the theological
     connotations of the word see Gunby, p. 445
169 *fore-winds* winds which blow the ship forward

[Act II, Scene iv]

Enter CAPUCHIN, ERCOLE *led between two* [SERVANTS]

CAPUCHIN

Look up sir,
You are preserved beyond natural reason:
You were brought dead out o'th'field, the surgeons
Ready to have embalmed you.

ERCOLE

I do look on my action with a thought of terror;   5
To do ill and dwell in't, is unmanly.

CAPUCHIN

You are divinely informed sir.

ERCOLE

I fought for one, in whom I have no more right,
Than false executors here in orphans' goods,
They cozen them of; yet though my cause were naught,   10
I rather chose the hazard of my soul,
Than forgo the compliment of a choleric man.

---

6 *dwell* persevere
7 *informed* inspired (Lucas)
12 *forgo the compliment* relinquish the reputation (Lucas)

This scene takes place in a street and is presented on the outer stage.
8–10 cf. Ben Jonson, *The Alchemist* (acted 1605–06; published 1607), II. v,
46–7, where Ananias described himself as
    . . . a seruant of the *exil'd Brethren*
    That deale with widdowes, and with orphanes goods;
The cheating of legatees by false executors who would make fraudulent
claims on their inheritances—often to the full value of the estates—
was a swindle of some antiquity described, for instance, in the *Profitable
Book* of Mr John Perkins, sometime Fellow of the Inner Temple, which
treated of the laws of England: a work which was first published in 1528
and, passing through Latin and French editions, was later published in
English and remained in print until 1827. The usefulness of the London
court in the 16th century in guarding orphans' goods from such fraudulent practices as well as from other inroads is illustrated by the account
given by Sir James Whitelocke of the way in which his mother, widowed
in 1570, guarded the interests of himself and three other small sons from
the unthriftiness and unkindness of her second husband, a merchant
called Thomas Price: 'by her extraordinarye providence and patience
did effect it, that she preserved in the handes of the city as orphans'
goods 600*l.*, for her fower suns everye of them 150*l.*, . . .' (Sir James
Whitelocke, *Liber Famelicus*, Camden Society, London, 1858, p. 6).

I pray continue the report of my death, and give out,
'Cause the church denied me Christian burial,
The vice-admiral of my galleys took my body,   15
With purpose to commit it to the earth,
Either in Sicil, or Malta.

CAPUCHIN   What aim you at
By this rumour of your death?

ERCOLE   There is hope of life
In Contarino; and he has my prayers
That he may live to enjoy what is his own,   20
The fair Jolenta; where, should it be thought
That I were breathing, happily her friends
Would oppose it still.

CAPUCHIN   But if you be supposed dead,
The law will strictly prosecute his life
For your murder.

ERCOLE   That's prevented thus: 25
There does belong a noble privilege
To all his family, ever since his father
Bore from the worthy Emperor Charles the Fifth
An answer to the French king's challenge, at such time
The two noble princes were engaged to fight,   30
Upon a frontier arm o'th' sea in a flat-bottomed boat,
That if any of his family should chance
To kill a man i'th' field, in a noble cause,
He should have his pardon; now sir, for his cause,
The world may judge if it were not honest.   35
Pray help me in speech, 'tis very painful to me.

CAPUCHIN
Sir I shall.

ERCOLE
The guilt of this lies in Romelio.
And as I hear, to second this good contract,
He has got a nun with child.

---

17 *Sicil* ed.: see Textual Appendix A
22 *happily* haply, perhaps
35 *honest* honourable

---

28 ff. Lucas points out that Webster is alluding here both to the famous
and abortive exchange of cartels between Francis I and Charles V, who
had accused the French king of a breach of faith, in 1528, and also to
another different challenge, to which Charles V made reference in 1536
when he claimed that he had challenged Francis I to fight with him, man
to man, in his shirt and in a boat: see Lucas, II, 337–8.

CAPUCHIN   There are crimes   40
  That either must make work for speedy repentance,
  Or for the devil.
ERCOLE   I have much compassion on him,
  For sin and shame are ever tied together
  With Gordian knots, of such a strong thread spun,
  They cannot without violence be undone.   45
                                                              Exeunt

                    Explicit Actus secundus

                Actus Tertius, Scena Prima

                    Enter ARIOSTO, CRISPIANO

ARIOSTO
  Well sir, now I must claim
  Your promise, to reveal to me the cause
  Why you live thus clouded.
CRISPIANO   Sir, the King of Spain
  Suspects that your Romelio here, the merchant
  Has discovered some gold-mine to his own use   5
  In the West Indies, and for that employs me
  To discover in what part of Christendom
  He vents this treasure. Besides, he is informed
  What mad tricks has been played of late by ladies.
ARIOSTO
  Most true, and I am glad the king has heard on't: 10

---

8 *vents* spends

    This scene probably takes place in the same location as II. iv.
40–2 cf. 'Newes of my morning worke' in Overbury's *Characters* (1614):
    'That sinne makes worke for repentance, or the Deuill' (Dent, p. 303).
44 *Gordian knots* Gordius was a Phrygian peasant who, in fulfilment of an
    oracle, became king of Phrygia. An oracle declared that whoever untied
    the cunning knot with which the yoke of Gordius' oxen was tied would
    become lord of Asia. The knot remained tied for centuries till Alexander,
    unable to untie it, severed it with his sword. Webster uses the same
    image of strength which only violence can break in *The Duchess of Malfi*,
    I. ii, 393–4, where the Duchess prays of her marriage contract with
    Antonio:
        Bless, Heaven, this sacred Gordian, which let violence
        Never untwine.

Why, they use their lords as if they were their wards;
And as your Dutchwomen in the Low Countries
Take all and pay all, and do keep their husbands
So silly all their lives of their own estates,
That when they are sick, and come to make their will,   15
They know not precisely what to give away
From their wives, because they know not what they are worth:
So here should I repeat what factions,
What bat-fowling for offices –
As you must conceive their game is all i'th' night –   20
What calling in question one another's honesties,
Withal what sway they bear i'th' viceroy's court,
You'd wonder at it:
'Twill do well shortly, can we keep them off
From being of our council of war.
CRISPIANO   Well, I have vowed   25
That I will never sit upon the bench more,
Unless it be to curb the insolencies
Of these women.
ARIOSTO   Well, take it on my word then,
Your place will not long be empty.   *Exeunt*

14 *silly . . . of* ignorant . . . about
19 *bat-fowling* catching roosting birds at night by dazzling them with
   torchlight and then stunning them with wooden bats; hence the
   term meant using dark practices to defraud the simple: see Lucas,
   II, 339
26 *bench* i.e., the judicial bench

11–17 Webster took his description of the behaviour of Dutch wives from
   Fynes Moryson's *Itinerary* (1617), Part III, Book IV, ch. 6: 'Take all
   and pay all' was a proverbial phrase, regularly applied to domineering
   wives. Webster had applied another common proverb to Dutchwomen
   in *The White Devil*, III. ii, 5–8 (Lucas, II, 338; Dent, pp. 102, 303 and
   Tilley, A 203).

[Act III, Scene ii]

Enter ROMELIO *in the habit of a Jew*

ROMELIO
    Excellently well habited! Why, methinks
    That I could play with mine own shadow now,
    And be a rare Italianated Jew;
    To have as many several change of faces
    As I have seen carved upon one cherrystone;   5
    To wind about a man like rotten ivy,
    Eat into him like quicksilver, poison a friend
    With pulling but a loose hair from's beard, or give a drench,
    He should linger of't nine years, and ne'er complain,
    But in the spring and fall, and so the cause   10
    Imputed to the disease natural; for slight villainies,
    As to coin money, corrupt ladies' honours,
    Betray a town to th' Turk, or make a bonefire
    O'th' Christian navy, I could settle to't
    As if I had eat a politician,   15
    And digested him to nothing but pure blood.
    But stay, I lose myself; this is the house.
    Within there!

[He knocks.] Enter two SURGEONS

FIRST SURGEON Now sir?
ROMELIO
    You are the men of art that, as I hear,
    Have the Lord Contarino under cure.   20
SECOND SURGEON
    Yes sir, we are his surgeons,

---

  1 s.d. *in the habit of a Jew* in the traditional Jewish gaberdine
  8 *drench* a dose of medicine
 11 *disease natural* ?discomfort caused by the change of season
 12 *coin* counterfeit
 13 *bonefire* bonfire
 14 *O'th'* ed. (A'th Q)
 15 *a politician* a crafty and intriguing schemer

This scene is also located in the street. The surgeons' house is within: that
is, on the inner stage.
    1 ff. For a discussion of the influence of Marlowe's *Jew of Malta* on the
      characterization of Romelio, especially in this scene, see Lucas, II,
      217–18, 339.

But he is past all cure.
ROMELIO   Why, is he dead?
FIRST SURGEON
He is speechless sir, and we do find his wound
So festered near the vitals, all our art
By warm drinks, cannot clear th'imposthumation,   25
And he's so weak, to make incision
By the orifix were present death to him.
ROMELIO
He has made a will I hear.
FIRST SURGEON   Yes sir.
ROMELIO
And deputed Jolenta his heir.
SECOND SURGEON   He has, we are witness to't.
ROMELIO
Has not Romelio been with you yet,   30
To give you thanks, and ample recompense
For the pains you have ta'en?
FIRST SURGEON   Not yet.
ROMELIO
Listen to me gentlemen, for I protest,
If you will seriously mind your own good,
I am come about a business shall convey   35
Large legacies from Contarino's will
To both of you.
SECOND SURGEON   How sir? Why Romelio
Has the will, and in that he has given us nothing.
ROMELIO
I pray attend me: I am a physician.
SECOND SURGEON
A physician? Where do you practise?   40
ROMELIO
In Rome.
FIRST SURGEON   Oh then you have store of patients.
ROMELIO
Store? Why look you, I can kill my twenty a month
And work but i' th' forenoons: – you will give me leave

25 *imposthumation* abscess   26 *make incision* Dyce (make Q)
27 *orifix* orifice, opening of the wound; *present* immediate
39 *attend* listen to; pay attention to

42–3 cf. Jonson, *Volpone* (acted 1605–06; published 1607), II. ii, 59–62
   where physicians are described as rogues who 'are able, very well, to
   kill their twentie a weeke, and play' (Dent, p. 303).

To jest and be merry with you; – but as I said,
All my study has been physic; I am sent   45
From a noble Roman that is near akin
To Contarino, and that ought indeed,
By the law of alliance, be his only heir,
To practise his good and yours.
BOTH SURGEONS   How, I pray sir?
ROMELIO
I can by an extraction which I have,   50
Though he were speechless, his eyes set in's head,
His pulses without motion, restore to him
For half an hour's space, the use of sense,
And perhaps a little speech: having done this,
If we can work him, as no doubt we shall,   55
To make another will, and therein assign
This gentleman his heir, I will assure you,
'Fore I depart this house, ten thousand ducats;
And then we'll pull the pillow from his head,
And let him e'en go whither the religion sends him   60
That he died in.
FIRST SURGEON   Will you give's ten thousand ducats?
ROMELIO
Upon my Jewism.
SECOND SURGEON   'Tis a bargain sir, we are yours.

   [*They go within, where they find*] CONTARINO *in a bed*

Here is the subject you must work on.
ROMELIO
Well said, you are honest men,
And go to the business roundly: but gentlemen,   65
I must use my art singly.
FIRST SURGEON   Oh sir, you shall have all privacy.

50 *extraction* extract; essence
62–3 s.d.: opposite l. 62a in Q
65 *roundly* justly
66 *singly* alone

59–61 There are parallels to these lines in *Volpone*, II. vi, 85–8; *Timon of
    Athens*, IV. iii, 32, and Donne's *Biathanatos*: see Dent, pp. 303–4.
62 *Upon my Jewism* an oath as false as Romelio's assumed disguise. cf. *As
    You Like It*, I. ii, 81: 'If you swear by that that is not, you are not
    forsworn'.

ROMELIO
  And the doors locked to me.
SECOND SURGEON   At your best pleasure.
  [*Aside*] Yet for all this, I will not trust this Jew.
FIRST SURGEON [*aside*]
    Faith, to say truth,
  I do not like him neither; he looks like a rogue.   70
  This is a fine toy, fetch a man to life,
  To make a new will; there's some trick in't.
  I'll be near you, Jew.   *Exeunt* SURGEONS
ROMELIO
  Excellent! As I would wish; these credulous fools
  Have given me freely what I would have bought   75
  With a great deal of money. – Softly, here's breath yet;
  Now Ercole, for part of the revenge,
  Which I have vowed for thy untimely death!
  Besides this politic working of my own,
  That scorns precedent; – why, should this great man live, 80
  And not enjoy my sister, as I have vowed
  He never shall, oh, he may alter's will
  Every new moon if he please; to prevent which,
  I must put in a strong caveat. Come forth then
  My desperate stiletto, that may be worn   85
  In a woman's hair, and ne'er discovered,
  And either would be taken for a bodkin
  Or a curling-iron at most; why, 'tis an engine
  That's only fit to put in execution
  Barmotho pigs! A most unmanly weapon,   90
  That steals into a man's life he knows not how:
  Oh that great Caesar, he that passed the shock
  Of so many armed pikes, and poisoned darts,
  Swords, slings, and battleaxes, should at length
  Sitting at ease on a cushion, come to die   95
  By such a shoemaker's awl as this, his soul let forth

74 *Excellent! As* ed. (Excellent as Q)
79 *Besides this* Dyce (Besides, this Q)
80 *why, should* Lucas (why should Q)
82 *shall,* Lucas (shall? Q)
84 *caveat* a process in court to suspend legal proceedings
85 *stiletto* a short dagger
88 *curling-iron* an instrument for curling hair; *engine* instrument
90 *Barmotho pigs* the Bermudas were famous in the 16th and 17th
   centuries for the multitude of their pigs
92 *that great* Dyce (great Q)

At a hole no bigger than the incision
Made for a wheal! Ud's foot, I am horribly angry,
That he should die so scurvily: yet wherefore
Do I condemn thee thereof so cruelly,   100
Yet shake him by the hand? 'Tis to express
That I would never have such weapons used,
But in a plot like this, that's treacherous.
Yet this shall prove most merciful to thee,
For it shall preserve thee   105
From dying on a public scaffold, and withal
Bring thee an absolute cure, thus.   *Stabs him*
                    So, 'tis done:
And now for my escape.

                    Enter SURGEONS

FIRST SURGEON   You rogue mountebank,
I will try whether your inwards can endure
To be washed in scalding lead.   110
ROMELIO
Hold! I turn Christian.
SECOND SURGEON
Nay, prithee be a Jew still;
I would not have a Christian be guilty
Of such a villainous act as this is.
ROMELIO
I am Romelio the merchant.   115
FIRST SURGEON
Romelio! You have proved yourself
A cunning merchant indeed.
ROMELIO   You may read why
I came hither.
SECOND SURGEON Yes, in a bloody Roman letter.
ROMELIO
I did hate this man, each minute of his breath
Was torture to me.
FIRST SURGEON   Had you forborne this act,   120

98 *wheal* pimple, pustule
101 *hand?* ed. (hand, Q)
107 *an absolute cure* i.e., as death is the end of all mortal ills
107 s.d.: opposite l. 107a in Q
109 *inwards* inside
117 *merchant* usual meaning; slang for 'fellow'
118 *a bloody Roman letter* a bloody letter from Rome, whence
    Romelio claims to come; a letter written in blood, in Roman type

4 * *

He had not lived this two hours.

ROMELIO   But he had died then,
And my revenge unsatisfied. Here's gold;
Never did wealthy man purchase the silence
Of a terrible scolding wife at a dearer rate,
Than I will pay for yours: here's your earnest   125
In a bag of double ducats.

SECOND SURGEON
Why look you sir, as I do weigh this business,
This cannot be counted murder in you by no means.
Why 'tis no more, than should I go and choke
An Irishman, that were three quarters drowned,   130
With pouring usquebaugh in's throat.

ROMELIO
You will be secret?

FIRST SURGEON   As your soul.

ROMELIO
The West Indies shall sooner want gold, than you then.

SECOND SURGEON
That protestation has the music of the mint in't.

ROMELIO [aside]
How unfortunately was I surprised!   135
I have made myself a slave perpetually
To these two beggars.   Exit

FIRST SURGEON
Excellent! By this act he has made his estate ours.

SECOND SURGEON
I'll presently grow a lazy surgeon, and ride on my foot-cloth;
I'll fetch from him every eight days a policy for a hundred   140
double ducats; if he grumble, I'll peach.

FIRST SURGEON
But let's take heed he do not poison us.

SECOND SURGEON
Oh, I will never eat nor drink with him,

125 *earnest* advance payment which secures the bargain
129 *than should I* than if I should
131 *usquebaugh* whiskey
139 *foot-cloth* see I. ii, 169n
140 *policy* i.e., the equivalent of a modern cheque
141 *peach* inform against [him]

127 *as I do weigh this business* 'no doubt, as he speaks, the Surgeon weighs
also the bag of ducats in his hand' (Lucas).

Without unicorn's horn in a hollow tooth.

CONTARINO
Oh!   145

FIRST SURGEON
Did he not groan?

SECOND SURGEON   Is the wind in that door still?

FIRST SURGEON
Ha! Come hither, note a strange accident:
His steel has lighted in the former wound,
And made free passage for the congealed blood;
Observe in what abundance it delivers   150
The putrefaction.

SECOND SURGEON   Methinks he fetches
His breath very lively.

FIRST SURGEON   The hand of heaven is in't,
That his intent to kill him should become
The very direct way to save his life.

SECOND SURGEON
Why, this is like one I have heard of in England,   155
Was cured o'th' gout, by being racked i'th' Tower.
Well, if we can recover him, here's reward
On both sides. Howsoever, we must be secret.

FIRST SURGEON
We are tied to't.

---

144 *unicorn's horn in a hollow tooth* i.e., in case the food or drink should be poisoned. The belief in the efficacy of unicorn's horn as an antidote to poison is as old as the legend of the unicorn itself. In the 16th century the supposed horn, both whole and powdered, was more expensive than gold. Moreover, both credence in the power of the horn and trade in whatever was supposed to represent it were fostered by unscrupulous doctors and apothecaries who included the ingredient in their prescriptions. In one case the power of unicorn's horn was said to be great enough to raise a man from death. See R. R. Cawley, *Unpathed Waters* (Princeton, 1940), p. 65.

146 *Is the wind in that door still?* Is that the way the wind blows? Lucas, II, 340–1 doubts if Webster intended the macabre effect in this line which Rupert Brooke saw in it (*John Webster and the Elizabethan Drama*, 1916, p. 109), but Dent disagrees: 'I think Webster probably intended a somewhat macabre effect, or at least a witty one, by his use of the old proverb; surely "wind" puns on the breathing of the revived Contarino' (Dent, p. 304). See Tilley, w 419.

155–6 Dent, p. 305, says that this was a topical allusion current about 1603. Parallels are to be found in *Volpone*, IV. vi, 32–3, Marston's *Malcontent*, III. i, 80–2, and a poem addressed to Sir Thomas Roe and once attributed to Donne.

When we cure gentlemen of foul diseases,   160
They give us so much for the cure, and twice as much,
That we do not blab on't. Come, let's to work roundly,
Heat the lotion, and bring the searing.

Exeunt

[Act III, Scene iii]

*A table set forth with two tapers, a death's head, a
book.* JOLENTA *in mourning,* ROMELIO *sits by her*

ROMELIO
Why do you grieve thus? Take a looking-glass,
And see if this sorrow become you; that pale face
Will make men think you used some art before,
Some odious painting. Contarino's dead.
JOLENTA
Oh, that he should die so soon!
ROMELIO   Why, I pray tell me,   5
Is not the shortest fever the best? And are not bad plays
The worse for their length?
JOLENTA   Add not to the ill y'ave done
An odious slander; he stuck i'th' eyes o'th' court.
As the most choice jewel there.
ROMELIO   Oh be not angry;
Indeed the court to well composed nature   10
Adds much to perfection: for it is, or should be,
As a bright crystal mirror to the world
To dress itself; but I must tell you, sister,
If th'excellency of the place could have wrought salvation,
The devil had ne'er fallen from heaven: he was proud, –   15

[JOLENTA *rises angrily, and seems about to go*]

Leave us, leave us?
Come, take you seat again: I have a plot,
If you will listen to it seriously,

162 *roundly* in a thoroughgoing manner
163 *the searing* the searing iron, used for cauterizing a wound
  1 s.d. *tapers* candles; *death's head* skull
  4 *painting* cosmetic
  8 *i'th' eyes o'th'* ed. (i'th eyes a'th Q)

This scene is set in a room in Leonora's house. At least the first part of
it is located on the inner stage.

That goes beyond example; it shall breed
Out of the death of these two noblemen,   20
The advancement of our house.
JOLENTA   Oh take heed,
A grave is a rotten foundation.
ROMELIO   Nay, nay, hear me.
'Tis somewhat indirectly, I confess:
But there is much advancement in the world,
That comes in indirectly. I pray mind me: 25
You are already made by absolute will
Contarino's heir: now if it can be proved
That you have issue by Lord Ercole,
I will make you inherit his land too.
JOLENTA   How's this?
Issue by him, he dead, and I a virgin!   30
ROMELIO
I knew you would wonder how it could be done,
But I have laid the case so radically,
Not all the lawyers in Christendom
Shall find any the least flaw in't. I have a mistress
Of the Order of St Clare, a beauteous nun,   35
Who being cloistered e'er she knew the heat
Her blood would arrive to, had only time enough
To repent, and idleness sufficient
To fall in love with me; and to be short,
I have so much disordered the holy Order,   40
I have got this nun with child.
JOLENTA   Excellent work
Made for a dumb midwife!
ROMELIO   I am glad you grow thus pleasant.
Now will I have you presently give out
That you are full two months quickened with child
By Ercole, which rumour can beget   45
No scandal to you, since we will affirm

31 *knew* ed. (know Q)
32 *laid* set forth, expounded; *radically* thoroughly

---

35 *the Order of St Clare* was founded by St Clare who had been professed
    by St Francis of Assisi in 1212. Strictly speaking, the order is the Second
    Order of St Francis, but the Rule generally accepted by it in 1253 was
    one of such poverty, austerity, and seclusion of life that the nuns are
    commonly known as the 'Poor Clares'. Angiolella's reaction to the
    austere life is understandable, if one could imagine the circumstances
    which may give Romelio access to her.

The precontract was so exactly done,
By the same words used in the form of marriage,
That with a little dispensation,
A money matter, it shall be registered   50
Absolute matrimony.

JOLENTA   So then, I conceive you,
My conceived child must prove your bastard.

ROMELIO   Right:
For at such time my mistress falls in labour,
You must feign the like.

JOLENTA   'Tis a pretty feat, this,
But I am not capable of it.

ROMELIO   Not capable?   55

JOLENTA
No, for the thing you would have me counterfeit
Is most essentially put in practice: nay, 'tis done,
I am with child already.

ROMELIO   Ha! By whom?

JOLENTA
By Contarino: do not knit the brow,
The precontract shall justify it, it shall: 60
Nay, I will get some singular fine churchman,
Or though he be a plural one, shall affirm,
He coupled us together.

ROMELIO   Oh misfortune!
Your child must then be reputed Ercole's.

JOLENTA
Your hopes are dashed then, since your votary's issue   65
Must not inherit the land.

ROMELIO   No matter for that,
So I preserve her fame. I am strangely puzzled:
Why, suppose that she be brought abed before you,
And we conceal her issue till the time
Of your delivery, and then give out   70
That you had two at a birth; ha, were't not excellent?

JOLENTA
And what resemblance, think you, would they have

57 *essentially* really   61 *singular* singularly
62 *plural* a priest holding more than one benefice simultaneously
65 *votary* nun

47–51 Romelio is referring to a contract *per verba de presenti:* 'by words
about the present'. This is the form of contract used by the Duchess of
Malfi to marry Antonio in *The Duchess of Malfi*, I. ii, 390 ff.: see above,
p. 21.

To one another? Twins are still alike:
But this is not your aim; you would have your child
Inherit Ercole's land. – Oh my sad soul,   75
Have you not made me yet wretched enough,
But after all this frosty age in youth,
Which you have witched upon me, you will seek
To poison my fame.

ROMELIO   That's done already.

JOLENTA
No sir, I did but feign it,   80
To a fatal purpose, as I thought.

ROMELIO   What purpose?

JOLENTA
If you had loved or tendered my dear honour,
You would have locked your poniard in my heart,
When I named I was with child; but I must live
To linger out, till the consumption   85
Of my own sorrow kill me.

ROMELIO [aside]   This will not do:
The devil has on the sudden furnished me
With a rare charm, yet a most unnatural falsehood:
No matter, so 'twill take.
Stay sister, I would utter to you a business,   90
But I am very loth: a thing indeed,
Nature would have compassionately concealed,
Till my mother's eyes be closed.

JOLENTA
Pray what's that sir?

ROMELIO   You did observe
With what a dear regard our mother tendered   95
The Lord Contarino, yet how passionately
She sought to cross the match: why this was merely
To blind the eye o'th' world; for she did know
That you would marry him, and he was capable.
My mother doted upon him, and it was plotted   100
Cunningly between them, after you were married,
Living all three together in one house,

73 *still* always   78 *witched* put upon by witchcraft
82 *tendered* been solicitous about
93 *closed* i.e., in death   99 *and he was capable* if he were fit

---

82–4 For comment on the significance of these lines for understanding
the relationship between Romelio and Jolenta see Elizabeth M. Brennan,
'The Relationship between Brother and Sister in the Plays of John
Webster', *MLR*, LVIII (1963), 489.

A thing I cannot whisper without horror:
Why, the malice scarce of devils would suggest,
Incontinence 'tween them two.

JOLENTA   I remember since his hurt,   105
She has been very passionately inquiring
After his health.

ROMELIO   Upon my soul, this jewel,
With a piece of the holy cross in't, this relic
Valued at many thousand crowns, she would have sent him,
Lying upon his death-bed.

JOLENTA   Professing, as you say,   110
Love to my mother: wherefore did he make
Me his heir?

ROMELIO
His will was made afore he went to fight,
When he was first a suitor to you.

JOLENTA
To fight: oh, well remembered!   115
If he loved my mother, wherefore did he lose
His life in my quarrel?

ROMELIO
For the affront sake, a word you understand not;
Because Ercole was pretended rival to him,
To clear your suspicion; I was gulled in't too;   120
Should he not have fought upon't, he had undergone
The censure of a coward.

JOLENTA
How came you by this wretched knowledge?

ROMELIO
His surgeon overheard it,
As he did sigh it out to his confessor,   125
Some half-hour 'fore he died.

JOLENTA
I would have the surgeon hanged
For abusing confession, and for making me
So wretched by th'report. Can this be truth?

ROMELIO
No, but direct falsehood,   130

117 *my quarrel* a quarrel about me

107–10 This relic has been previously mentioned at II. iii, 148–51.

130 *falsehood* As Lucas points out, it is important, for the understanding of
the play, to realize that Romelio does not know that Leonora really does
love Contarino, though she is innocent of any plot with Contarino
against Jolenta (Lucas, II, 341).

As ever was banished the court. Did you ever hear
Of a mother that has kept her daughter's husband
For her own tooth? He fancied you in one kind,
For his lust,
And he loved our mother in another kind,   135
For her money:
The gallant's fashion right. But come, ne'er think on't,
Throw the fowl to the devil that hatched it, and let this
Bury all ill that's in't; she is our mother.

JOLENTA
I never did find anything i'th' world   140
Turn my blood so much as this: here's such a conflict
Between apparent presumption and unbelief
That I shall die in't.
Oh, if there be another world i'th' moon,
As some fantastics dream, I could wish all men,   145
The whole race of them, for their inconstancy,
Sent thither to people that. Why, I protest,
I now affect the Lord Ercole's memory
Better than the other's.

ROMELIO
But were Contarino living, –

JOLENTA   I do call any thing to witness,   150
That the divine law prescribed us to strengthen
An oath, were he living and in health, I would never
Marry with him. Nay, since I have found the world

137 *right* exactly
138 *fowl* (i) bird; (ii) foul; this seems to be a variant of the proverb
     (Tilley, B 376) 'An ill bird lays an ill egg'
142 *apparent* manifest
148 *affect* feel a preference for

144–5 cf. *The Duchess of Malfi*, II. iv, 16–19. Contemporary science popular-
       ized references to *another world i'th' moon* at this time: see Dent,
       pp. 305–6.
150–2 Divine law did not prescribe particular forms of oaths, but it did
       proscribe some: see St Matthew, v, 34–6. Moreover, the law of Jacobean
       England imposed penalties on swearers. The *Act to Restrain Abuses of
       Players*, passed in 1606, imposed a £10 fine 'for any profane or jesting
       use of the names of God, Christ Jesus, the Holy Ghost, or the Trinity,
       in any stage play, interlude, show, May-game, or pageant'. There is
       reason to believe that, in deference to this law's demands, Webster
       substituted 'Heaven' for 'God' in the text of *The Duchess of Malfi*:
       see G. P. V. Akrigg, 'The Name of God and *The Duchess of Malfi*',
       N&Q, CXLV (1950), 231–3.

So false to me, I'll be as false to it:
I will mother this child for you.
ROMELIO   Ha?   155
JOLENTA
Most certainly it will beguile part of my sorrow.
ROMELIO
Oh most assuredly; make you smile to think
How many times i'th' world lordships descend
To divers men that might, and truth were known,
Be heir, for any thing belongs to th' flesh,   160
As well to the Turk's richest eunuch.
JOLENTA   But do you not think
I shall have a horrible strong breath now?
ROMELIO   Why?
JOLENTA
Oh, with keeping your counsel, 'tis so terrible foul.
ROMELIO
Come, come, come,
You must leave these bitter flashes.   165
JOLENTA
Must I dissemble dishonesty? You have divers
Counterfeit honesty: but I hope here's none
Will take exceptions; I now must practise
The art of a great-bellied woman, and go feign
Their qualms and swoundings.
ROMELIO   Eat unripe fruit, and oatmeal,   170
To take away your colour.
JOLENTA   Dine in my bed
Some two hours after noon.
ROMELIO   And when you are up,
Make to your petticoat a quilted preface,

159 *and truth* if truth
160 *for . . . flesh* 'for aught that physical relationship has to do with
      it' (Lucas)
161 *the Turk's* i.e., the great Turk's   166 *dishonesty* unchastity
167 *honesty* (i) usual meaning; (ii) chastity
170 *qualms* (sudden) feelings of faintness or sickness
      swoundings swoonings
173 *preface* i.e., a layer added to the front of the petticoat; also
      alluding to the preface which recommends ('advances') a book

161-3 an idea of frequent occurrence in English works as well as in Erasmus,
       Manutius, and Guazzo: see Dent, p. 306.
168-74 The style and content of this passage recall *The White Devil*, III. iii,
        71 ff.

To advance your belly.

JOLENTA   I have a strange conceit now.
I have known some women when they were with child,   175
Have longed to beat their husbands: what if I,
To keep decorum, exercise my longing
Upon my tailor that way, and noddle him soundly,
He'll make the larger bill for't.

ROMELIO
I'll get one shall be as tractable to't as stockfish.   180

JOLENTA
Oh my fantastical sorrow! Cannot I now
Be miserable enough, unless I wear
A pied fool's coat? Nay worse, for when our passions
Such giddy and uncertain changes breed,
We are never well, till we are mad indeed.   *Exit* 185

ROMELIO
So: nothing in the world could have done this,
But to beget in her a strong distaste
Of the Lord Contarino: oh jealousy,
How violent, especially in women,
How often has it raised the devil up   190
In form of a law-case! My especial care
Must be, to nourish craftily this fiend
'Tween the mother and the daughter, that the deceit
Be not perceived. My next task, that my sister,
After this supposed childbirth, be persuaded   195
To enter into religion: 'tis concluded,
She must never marry; so I am left guardian
To her estate: and lastly, that my two surgeons
Be waged to the East Indies: let them prate
When they are beyond the line; the calenture,   200

174 *advance* put forward   178 *noddle* pummel on the head
180 *as tractable to't as stockfish* to beat someone 'like a stockfish' was
     a proverbial phrase (see Tilley, S 867); stockfish was hard dried
     haddock, cod, or other fish which had to be beaten before cooking
     to make it palatable
193 *the deceit* i.e., his story of Leonora's plan to deceive Jolenta with
     Contarino
196 *To enter into religion* to enter a religious order
199 *waged to the East Indies* hired to go to the East Indies, possibly as
     surgeons on one of Romelio's trading vessels
200 *the line* the equinoctial line, the equator; *calenture* 'a disease
     supposed to attack voyagers in tropical seas and make them try
     to jump in their delirium into the sea, imagining it to be green
     fields' (Lucas)

Or the scurvy, or the Indian pox, I hope,
Will take order for their coming back.

Enter LEON[ORA]

Oh here's my mother. I ha' strange news for you;
My sister is with child.
LEONORA   I do look now
For some great misfortunes to follow: for indeed mischiefs   205
Are like the visits of Franciscan friars,
They never come to pray upon us single.
In what estate left you Contarino?
ROMELIO   Strange, that you
Can skip from the former sorrow to such a question!
I'll tell you: in the absence of his surgeon,   210
My charity did that for him in a trice,
They would have done at leisure, and been paid for't.
I have killed him.
LEONORA   I am twenty years elder
Since you last opened your lips.
ROMELIO   Ha?
LEONORA
You have given him the wound you speak of,   215
Quite thorough your mother's heart.
ROMELIO
I will heal it presently mother: for this sorrow
Belongs to your error: you would have him live
Because you think he's father of the child;
But Jolenta vows by all the rights of truth,   220
'Tis Ercole's. It makes me smile to think

201 *scurvy* a disease common to sailors, caused by Vitamin C
    deficiency
206–7 Franciscans travelled in pairs; there is a pun on pray and prey
216 *thorough* through
217 *presently* immediately

---

201 *the Indian pox* i.e., syphilis, was erroneously believed to have originated
    among American Indians and to have been spread by cannibalism. Sir
    Thomas Browne refers to this theory in 'Of the Blackness of Negroes',
    Pseudodoxia Epidemica (1616), Book VI, ch. 10, 328: 'How the venereall
    contagion began in that part of the earth, [i.e., America] since history is
    silent, is not easily resolved by Philosophy; For, whereas it is imputed
    unto Anthropophagy, or the eating of mans flesh, the cause hath beene
    common unto many other Countries, and there have beene Canibals or
    men-eaters in the three other parts of the world, if wee credit the re-
    lations of Ptolomy, Strabo, and Pliny'.

How cunningly my sister could be drawn
To the contract, and yet how familiarly
To his bed. Doves never couple without
A kind of murmur.
LEONORA   Oh, I am very sick.   225
ROMELIO
Your old disease: when you are grieved, you are troubled
With the mother.
LEONORA [*aside*]   I am rapt with the mother indeed,
That I ever bore such a son.
ROMELIO   Pray tend my sister;
I am infinitely full of business.
LEONORA   Stay, you will mourn
For Contarino?
ROMELIO   Oh by all means, 'tis fit: 230
My sister is his heir.   *Exit*
LEONORA
I will make you chief mourner, believe it.
Never was woe like mine: oh, that my care
And absolute study to preserve his life,
Should be his absolute ruin! Is he gone then?   235
There is no plague i'th' world can be compared
To impossible desire, for they are plagued
In the desire itself: never, oh never
Shall I behold him living, in whose life
I lived far sweetlier than in mine own.   240
A precise curiosity has undone me; why did I not
Make my love known directly? 'T had not been
Beyond example, for a matron to affect
I'th' honourable way of marriage,
So youthful a person: oh I shall run mad: 245
For as we love our youngest children best,

222 i.e., 'what cunning she forced me to use in order to draw her, how
     cunningly she had to be drawn' (Lucas)
227 *the mother* hysterical passion, characterized by a rising feeling
     in the stomach; being a mother; *rapt* carried away
237 *they* i.e., those who are tormented with impossible desire
241 *precise curiosity* 'over-scrupulous nicety of behaviour' (Lucas)

236–8 from *Arcadia*, II, iv where Philoclea laments the impossibility of her
     love for Zelmane: 'it is the impossibilitie that dooth torment me: for,
     unlawfull desires are punished after the effect of enjoying; but un-
     possible desires are punished in the desire it selfe. [It is] ... of all
     despaires the most miserable, which is drawn from impossibilitie' (Dent,
     p. 307).

So the last fruit of our affection,
Wherever we bestow it, is most strong,
Most violent, most unresistible,
Since 'tis indeed our latest harvest-home,   250
Last merriment 'fore winter; and we widows,
As men report of our best picture-makers,
We love the piece we are in hand with better
Than all the excellent work we have done before.
And my son has deprived me of all this. Ha, my son!   255
I'll be a fury to him; like an Amazon lady,
I'd cut off this right pap, that gave him suck,
To shoot him dead. I'll no more tender him
Than had a wolf stolen to my teat i'th' night,
And robbed me of my milk: nay, such a creature   260
I should love better far. – Ha, ha, what say you?
I do talk to somewhat, methinks; it may be
My evil genius. Do not the bells ring?
I have a strange noise in my head: oh, fly in pieces!
Come age, and wither me into the malice   265
Of those that have been happy; let me have
One property more than the devil of hell,
Let me envy the pleasure of youth heartily,
Let me in this life fear no kind of ill,
That have no good to hope for: let me die   270
In the distraction of that worthy princess,

---

250 *latest* last; *harvest-home* conclusion of harvesting and its accompanying celebration
257 *this right* Qb (his right Qa)
264 *fly in pieces* i.e., like an overcharged cannon: cf. *The Duchess of Malfi*, III. v, 102–3

256–7 Legends concerning the warrior women known as Amazons are found in literature from Homer onwards. It was supposed that the right breast was amputated (or cauterized at birth) to enable them to use their bows more efficiently.

271 ff. Lucas sees here a clear allusion to the romantic story of Queen Elizabeth's mourning for the Earl of Essex after his execution. Her grief was exacerbated by the discovery that, contrary to her belief, Essex had sued to her for pardon, sending to her a ring which she had once given him with the promise that, should he ever send it to her, his sins against her would be forgiven. The ring had been given to a boy to deliver to Lady Scrope to present to the queen, but the boy had mistakenly given it to her sister, the Countess of Nottingham, whose husband forbade her to deal in the matter. See Lucas, II, 343–4.

Who loathed food, and sleep, and ceremony,
For thought of losing that brave gentleman,
She would fain have saved, had not a false conveyance
Expressed him stubborn-hearted. Let me sink   275
Where neither man, nor memory may ever find me.

Falls down. [*Enter* CAPUCHIN *with* ERCOLE, *who remains in the
background*]

CAPUCHIN
This is a private way which I command,
As her confessor. I would not have you seen yet,
Till I prepare her. Peace to you, lady.

LEONORA   Ha?

CAPUCHIN
You are well employed, I hope; the best pillow i'th' world   280
For this your contemplation, is the earth,
And the best object, heaven.

LEONORA
I am whispering to a dead friend.

CAPUCHIN   And I am come
To bring tidings of a friend was dead,
Restored to life again.

LEONORA   Say sir?   285

CAPUCHIN
One whom I dare presume, next to your children,
You tendered above life.

LEONORA   Heaven will not suffer me
Utterly to be lost.

CAPUCHIN   For he should have been
Your son-in-law: miraculously saved,
When surgery gave him o'er.

LEONORA   Oh, may you live   290
To win many souls to heaven, worthy sir,
That your crown may be the greater. Why, my son
Made me believe he stole into his chamber,
And ended that which Ercole began
By a deadly stab in's heart.

ERCOLE [*aside*]   Alas, she mistakes!   295

---

275 *Expressed him stubborn-hearted* Qb (not in Qa) gave the impression
    that he was stubborn-hearted
284 *was dead* Qb (not dead Qa)
285 *Say sir?* What do you say sir?

'Tis Contarino she wishes living; but I must fasten
On her last words, for my own safety.
LEONORA   Where,
Oh where shall I meet this comfort?
ERCOLE [*coming forward*]
Here in the vowed consort of your daughter.
LEONORA
Oh I am dead again: instead of the man, you present me   300
The grave swallowed him.
ERCOLE   Collect yourself, good lady.
Would you behold brave Contarino living?
There cannot be a nobler chronicle
Of his good than myself: if you would view him dead,
I will present him to you bleeding fresh,   305
In my penitency.
LEONORA   Sir, you do only live
To redeem another ill you have committed,
That my poor innocent daughter perish not
By your vild sin, whom you have got with child.
ERCOLE
Here begin all my compassion: oh poor soul!   310
She is with child by Contarino; and he dead,
By whom should she preserve her fame to th' world,
But by myself that loved her 'bove the world?
There never was a way more honourable
To exercise my virtue, than to father it,   315
And preserve her credit, and to marry her.
I'll suppose her Contarino's widow, bequeathed to me
Upon his death: for sure she was his wife,
But that the ceremony o'th' church was wanting.

296–7 i.e., Ercole must make use of Leonora's revelation of Romelio's
        attempt on Contarino's life
299 *vowed consort* Lucas's conjecture (vowed comfort Q) betrothed
        consort

───

309 *vild sin* Leonora takes the attitude of an outraged matron, her piety no
        doubt tinged by consciousness of her own yearning for Contarino. Jolenta
        had alleged that precontract justified pregnancy: see III. iii, 60. The
        difference in opinion is the result of differences between the strict
        religious disapproval both of cohabitation before marriage and of
        irregular marriages (i.e., those performed outside the Church) and
        common practice—supported to some extent by the law—which justi-
        fied cohabitation and allowed for the consummation of a betrothal to be
        considered as valid marriage. cf. *The Duchess of Malfi*, and *Measure for
        Measure*.

Report this to her, madam, and withal　　　　　　320
That never father did conceive more joy
For the birth of an heir, than I to understand
She had such confidence in me. I will not now
Press a visit upon her, till you have prepared her:
For I do read in your distraction,　　　　　　　325
Should I be brought o'th' sudden to her presence,
Either the hasty fright, or else the shame
May blast the fruit within her. I will leave you
To commend as loyal faith and service to her
As e'er heart harboured: by my hope of bliss,　　330
I never lived to do good act but this.

CAPUCHIN [*aside*]
Withal, and you be wise,
Remember what the mother has revealed
Of Romelio's treachery.　　　　　*Exeunt* ERCOLE, CAPUCHIN

LEONORA
A most noble fellow! In his loyalty　　　　　　335
I read what worthy comforts I have lost
In my dear Contarino, and all adds
To my despair. —— Within there!

Enter WINIFRED

　　　　　　　　　　　　Fetch the picture
Hangs in my inner closet.　　　　*Exit* WIN[IFRED]
　　　　　　　　　I remember,
I let a word slip of Romelio's practice　　　　　340
At the surgeons': no matter, I can salve it;
I have deeper vengeance that's preparing for him.
To let him live and kill him: that's revenge
I meditate upon.

Enter WIN[IFRED *with*] *the picture*

　　　　　　　So, hang it up.
I was enjoined by the party ought that picture,　　345
Forty years since, ever when I was vexed,

332 *and you* if you
335 *fellow! In his loyalty* ed. (fellow in his loyalty. Q)
338 s.d.: opposite l. 338a in Q
339 s.d.: opposite l. 340 in Q
340 *practice* treachery, trickery
341 *salve* salvage, repair
344 s.d.: WIN[IFRED *with*] ed. (*Win. and* Q)
345 *ought* who owned

To look upon that: what was his meaning in't
I know not, but methinks upon the sudden
It has furnished me with mischief, such a plot
As never mother dreamt of. Here begins   350
My part i'th' play: my son's estate is sunk
By loss at sea, and he has nothing left,
But the land his father left him. 'Tis concluded,
The law shall undo him. Come hither,
I have a weighty secret to impart,   355
But I would have thee first confirm to me,
How I may trust that thou canst keep my counsel
Beyond death.

WINIFRED   Why mistress, 'tis your only way,
To enjoin me first that I reveal to you
The worst act I e'er did in all my life: 360
So one secret shall bind another.

LEONORA   Thou instruct'st me
Most ingenuously; for indeed it is not fit,
Where any act is plotted, that is naught,
Any of counsel to it should be good,
And in a thousand ills have happed i'th' world,   365
The intelligence of one another's shame
Have wrought far more effectually than the tie
Of conscience, or religion.

WINIFRED   But think not, mistress,
That any sin which ever I committed
Did concern you; for proving false in one thing,   370
You were a fool, if ever you would trust me
In the least matter of weight.

LEONORA   Thou hast lived with me
These forty years; we have grown old together,
As many ladies and their women do,
With talking nothing, and with doing less: 375
We have spent our life in that which least concerns life,
Only in putting on our clothes; and now I think on't,
I have been a very courtly mistress to thee,
I have given thee good words, but no deeds; now's the time
To requite all: my son has six lordships left him.   380

361 *another* Hazlitt, Lucas (one another Q, Dyce)
362 *ingenuously* ingeniously
363 *naught* good-for-nothing; wicked
366 *intelligence* knowledge
378 *courtly* like a courtier

WINIFRED
  'Tis truth.
LEONORA   But he cannot live four days to enjoy them.
WINIFRED
  Have you poisoned him?
LEONORA   No, the poison is yet but brewing.
WINIFRED
  You must minister it to him with all privacy.
LEONORA
  Privacy? It shall be given him
  In open court; I'll make him swallow it   385
  Before the judge's face: if he be master
  Of poor ten arpines of land forty hours longer,
  Let the world repute me an honest woman.
WINIFRED
  So 'twill, I hope.
LEONORA   Oh thou canst not conceive
  My unimitable plot! Let's to my ghostly father,   390
  Where first I will have thee make a promise
  To keep my counsel, and then I will employ thee
  In such a subtle combination,
  Which will require, to make the practice fit,
  Four devils, five advocates, to one woman's wit.   395
                                                    Exeunt

                    Explicit Actus Tertius

383 *minister* administer
387 *arpines* arpents: an arpent was an old French land measure,
     roughly equivalent to an acre
388 *honest* chaste
390 *ghostly* spiritual
394 *practice* see III. iii, 340n
395 *advocates* ed. (Qa Aduocates; Qb Aduocats); *one* Qb (a Qa)

Actus Quartus, Scena Prima

Enter LEONORA, SANITONELLA *at one door,* [*with*] WINIFRED,
REGISTER: *at the other,* ARIOSTO

SANITONELLA [*to* REGISTER]
    Take her into your office sir; she has that in her belly,
    Will dry up your ink, I can tell you.
                  [*Exeunt* REGISTER *and* WINIFRED]
    This is the man that is your learned counsel,
    A fellow that will troll it off with tongue:
    He never goes without restorative powder   5
    Of the lungs of fox in's pocket, and Malaga raisins
    To make him long-winded. Sir, this gentlewoman
    Entreats your counsel in an honest cause,
    Which please you sir, this brief, my own poor labour,
    Will give you light of.   [*He gives the brief to* ARIOSTO]
ARIOSTO   Do you call this a brief?   10
    Here's as I weigh them, some four-score sheets of paper.
    What would they weigh if there were cheese wrapped in
        them,
    Or fig-dates?
SANITONELLA   Joy come to you, you are merry:
    We call this but a brief in our office.
    The scope of the business lies i'th' margin.   15
ARIOSTO
    Methinks you prate too much.
    I never could endure an honest cause
    With a long prologue to't.
LEONORA   You trouble him.
ARIOSTO
    What's here? Oh strange; I have lived this sixty years,

4 *troll* to move the tongue volubly
10 *a brief* a lawyer's statement of the facts of a case which should,
    literally, be brief; Sanitonella's obviously isn't
13 *fig-dates* fig-dotes: wild figs; an inferior kind of fig
15 *i'th' margin* ed. (ith Margent sheet Qa; i'th Margent Qb)

The scene is located in the antechamber of a Neapolitan law court
and occupies the outer stage.
  6 *lungs of fox* 'used, by a sort of sympathetic magic, for consumption,
    asthma, and other lung diseases' (Lucas, II, 345); *Malaga raisins* ed.
    (Malligo Reasins Q) raisins from Malaga, in southern Spain, a port
    famous for its export of white wine. Raisins were prescribed medicinally
    for hoarseness, shortness of breath, or difficulty in breathing (ibid.).

Yet in my practice never did shake hands   20
With a cause so odious. Sirrah, are you her knave?

SANITONELLA
No sir, I am a clerk.

ARIOSTO   Why you whoreson fogging rascal,
Are there not whores enough for presentations,
Of overseers, wrong the will o'th' dead,
Oppressions of widows, or young orphans,   25
Wicked divorces, or your vicious cause
Of *plus quam satis*, to content a woman,
But you must find new stratagems, new pursenets?
Oh women, as the ballad lives to tell you,
What will you shortly come to?   30

SANITONELLA
Your fee is ready sir.

ARIOSTO   The devil take such fees,
And all such suits i'th' tail of them! See, the slave
Has writ false Latin: sirrah Ignoramus,
Were you ever at the university?

SANITONELLA   Never sir:
But 'tis well known to divers I have commenced   35
In a pew of our office.

ARIOSTO   Where, in a pew of your office?

---

20 *shake hands* i.e., meet   21 *knave* servant
23 *presentations* presentments, i.e., acts of presenting before a court
   a formal statement of a matter to be dealt with legally
24 *Of overseers, wrong* of executors enough, who wrong: see II. iv,
   8–10n
26 *divorces* Qb (Diuerses Qa)
27 *plus quam satis* more than enough: possibly a comic variation of
   nunquam satis—by no means enough—a legal tag apparently used
   in suits for annulment of marriage (Lucas, II, 346)
28 *pursenets* Qb (pursuits Qa) bag-shaped nets whose mouths were
   closed by a draw-string; hence, traps
32 *them* Qb (thee Qa)
33 *Ignoramus* Qb (Ignorance Qa)
35 *But 'tis* Qb (It is Qa); *commenced* technical term for proceeding to
   a degree
36 *pew* raised seat or bench

---

22 *fogging* pettifogging: 'fogger' derived from Fugger, the surname of the
   Augsburg merchants and financiers who were famous in the 15th and
   16th centuries. A 'petty fogger' would mean a small-scale swindler;
   fogging or pettifogging came to be particularly applied as an oppro-
   brious epithet to lawyers of a low class.

SANITONELLA

I have been dry-foundered in't this four years,
Seldom found non-resident from my desk.

ARIOSTO

Non-resident subsummer!
I'll tear your libel for abusing that word,   40
By virtue of the clergy.   *[Tears up the brief]*

SANITONELLA   What do you mean sir?
It cost me four nights' labour.

ARIOSTO   Hadst thou been drunk
So long, th'hadst done our court better service.

LEONORA   Sir,
You do forget your gravity, methinks.

ARIOSTO

Cry ye mercy, do I so?   45
And as I take it, you do very little remember
Either womanhood, or Christianity.
Why do ye meddle
With that seducing knave, that's good for naught,
Unless 't be to fill the office full of fleas,   50
Or a winter itch; wears that spacious ink-horn
All a vacation only to cure tetters,
And his penknife to weed corns from the splay toes
Of the right worshipful of the office?

37 *dry-foundered* a farrier's term applied to horses lamed from in-
flammation of the hoof caused by overwork; hence, worked to a
standstill

38 *non-resident* a term applied to a priest who retained a benefice
without being resident in the parish

39 *subsumner* a summoner delivered summonses to appear in court,
and so '*sub*-summoner is clearly meant to convey the extremity
of contempt' (Lucas)

40 *libel* written statement of the plaintiff's case which institutes his
lawsuit

43 *th'hadst* ed. (T'hadst Q; Thou'dst Dyce; Th'hadst Hazlitt; th'adst
Lucas)

51 *winter itch* '*pruritus hiemalis*, an obscure disease tending to
reappear each winter on the sufferer's exposure to cold' (Lucas);
ink-horn small portable vessel for carrying ink

52 *tetters* eruptive skin disease: ink, containing tannic acid, would
be efficacious in curing it

53 *splay toes* toes which spread outwards

LEONORA
  You make bold with me, sir.   55
ARIOSTO
  Woman, y'are mad, I'll swear't, and have more need
  Of a physician than a lawyer.
  The melancholy humour flows in your face,
  Your painting cannot hide it: such vild suits
  Disgrace our courts, and these make honest lawyers   60
  Stop their own ears, whilst they plead and that's the reason
  Your younger men that have good conscience
  Wear such large nightcaps: go old woman, go pray
  For lunacy, or else the devil himself
  Has ta'en possession of thee; may like cause   65
  In any Christian court never find name:
  Bad suits, and not the law, bred the law's shame. *Exit*
LEONORA
  Sure the old man's frantic.
SANITONELLA   Plague on's gouty fingers!
  Were all of his mind, to entertain no suits
  But such they thought were honest, sure our lawyers   70
  Would not purchase half so fast.

Enter CONTILUPO, *a spruce lawyer*

                But here's the man,
  Learned Signior Contilupo, here's a fellow
  Of another piece, believe't; I must make shift
  With the foul copy.   [*He approaches* CONTILUPO]
CONTILUPO   Business to me?
SANITONELLA
  To you sir, from this lady.
CONTILUPO   She is welcome.   75
SANITONELLA
  'Tis a foul copy sir, you'll hardly read it, –
  There's twenty double ducats, – can you read sir?
CONTILUPO
  Exceeding well; very, very exceeding well.

---

59 *vild* vile
63 *nightcaps* white coifs worn by sergeants at law: cf. II. i, 41n
71 *purchase* make a profit; s.d.: opposite l. 71b in Q
74 *foul copy* rough draft of the brief

SANITONELLA
    This man will be saved, he can read; Lord, Lord,
    To see what money can do; be the hand never so foul,   80
    Somewhat will be picked out on't.
CONTILUPO   Is not this
    'Vivere honeste'?
SANITONELLA   No, that's struck out sir;
    And wherever you find 'Vivere honeste' in these papers
    Give it a dash sir.
CONTILUPO   I shall be mindful of it.
    In troth you write a pretty secretary;   85
    Your secretary hand ever takes best in mine opinion.
SANITONELLA
    Sir, I have been in France,
    And there, believe't, your court hand generally
    Takes beyond thought.
CONTILUPO   Even as a man is traded in't.
SANITONELLA
    That I could not think of this virtuous gentleman   90
    Before I went to th'tother hog-rubber!
    Why, this was wont to give young clerks half fees,
    To help him to clients. Your opinion in the case, sir?

80–1 (i) something can be made out from the worst handwriting; (ii)
      some gain can be made from the dirtiest hand (Lucas)
81 *on't* of it
82–3 'Vivere honeste' ed. (*Viuere honeste* Q) to live honestly
      (chastely)
83 *wherever* ed. (where euer Q),
84 *Give it a dash* stroke it out
85–6 *secretary hand* the style of handwriting commonly used
      between the 15th and 17th centuries
88 *court hand* the style of writing used specifically in English law
      courts between the 16th and 18th centuries; it was less legible
      than secretary hand
89 *traded* practised
91 *hog-rubber* term of abuse for a rustic or unrefined person

79 *This man will be saved, he can read* a reference to the fact that, by plead-
    ing benefit of clergy (i.e., learning) a man could claim exemption from
    first conviction for certain offences. The usual test applied was ability to
    read, in Latin and black letter, the beginning of Psalm li, which thus
    became known as the 'neck-verse' because reading it could save a
    man's neck. Ben Jonson, having killed a fellow actor in a duel, pleaded
    benefit of clergy and the death sentence was commuted to branding in
    the thumb.

CONTILUPO
I am struck with wonder, almost extasied,
With this most goodly suit.   95
LEONORA
It is the fruit of a most hearty penitence.
CONTILUPO
'Tis a case shall leave a precedent to all the world,
In our succeeding annals, and deserves
Rather a spacious public theatre,
Than a pent court for audience; it shall teach   100
All ladies the right path to rectify their issue.
SANITONELLA
Lo you, here's a man of comfort.
CONTILUPO
And you shall go unto a peaceful grave,
Discharged of such a guilt, as would have lain
Howling for ever at your wounded heart,   105
And rose with you to Judgement.
SANITONELLA
Oh give me such a lawyer, as will think
Of the Day of Judgement!
LEONORA
You must urge the business against him
As spitefully as may be.   110
CONTILUPO
Doubt not. What, is he summoned?
SANITONELLA
Yes, and the court will sit within this half hour.
Peruse your notes, you have very short warning.
CONTILUPO
Never fear you that.
Follow me, worthy lady, and make account   115
This suit is ended already.   *Exeunt*

94 *extasied* enraptured
100 *pent* confined

[Act IV, Scene ii]

Enter OFFICERS *preparing seats for the Judges, to them* ERCOLE
muffled

FIRST OFFICER

You would have a private seat sir?

ERCOLE

Yes sir.

SECOND OFFICER

Here's a closet belongs to th' court,

Where you may hear all unseen.

ERCOLE

I thank you; there's money.   5

SECOND OFFICER

I give you your thanks again sir.

Enter CONTARINO, *the* SURGEONS, *disguised*

CONTARINO

Is't possible Romelio's persuaded,

You are gone to the East Indies?

FIRST SURGEON   Most confidently.

CONTARINO

But do you mean to go?

SECOND SURGEON   How? Go to the East Indies?

And so many Hollanders gone to fetch sauce for their   10

pickled herrings; some have been peppered there too lately.

But I pray, being thus well recovered of your wounds, why

do you not reveal yourself?

CONTARINO

That my fair Jolenta should be rumoured

To be with child by noble Ercole   15

Makes me expect to what a violent issue

These passages will come. I hear her brother

Is marrying the infant she goes with,

6 s.d.: opposite ll. 3–4 in Q; Contarino is disguised as a Dane: see
  ll. 570–1 and V. iv, 5

This scene, set in the Neapolitan law court, utilizes the whole stage. Lucas
comments that it is 'surely one of the vividest scenes in all Elizabethan
drama' (II, 349).

11 *some have been peppered there too lately* a general or particular reference
   to the hostilities between the Dutch and English in the East Indies.
   This passage has been used by some scholars in attempts to date the
   play precisely: see Lucas, II, 214.

Fore it be born: as, if it be a daughter,
To the Duke of Austria's nephew; if a son,   20
Into the noble ancient family
Of the Palavifini. He's a subtle devil.
And I do wonder what strange suit in law,
Has happed between him and's mother.
FIRST SURGEON   'Tis whispered
     'mong the lawyers,
'Twill undo him for ever. *Enter* SANIT[ONELLA,] WIN[IFRED]
SANITONELLA   Do you hear, officers?   25
You must take special care, that you let in
No brachygraphy men, to take notes.
FIRST OFFICER   No sir?
SANITONELLA   By no means,
We cannot have a cause of any fame,
But you must have scurvy pamphlets, and lewd ballads
Engendered of it presently. Have you broke fast yet?
WINIFRED   Not I
     sir.   30
SANITONELLA
'Twas very ill done of you:
For this cause will be long a-pleading; but no matter,
I have a modicum in my buckram bag,
To stop your stomach.   What is't? Green ginger?
WINIFRED
SANITONELLA
Green ginger, nor pellitory of Spain neither,   35
Yet 'twill stop a hollow tooth better than either of them.
WINIFRED
Pray what is't?
SANITONELLA   Look you, [*opens his bag and brings out a pie*]
It is a very lovely pudding-pie,

22 *Palavifini* probably the Pallavicini, a noble Italian family which
   had English connections in the late 16th century
25 s.d. in margin opposite l. 25a in Q
27 *brachygraphy men* writers of shorthand: such men used to take
   shorthand notes of Elizabethan plays, in the theatre, which
   formed the bases of pirated editions, issued by unscrupulous
   printers
30 *presently* immediately; *Have* Dyce, Hazlitt (SAN. Have Q, Lucas)
33 *modicum* small quantity of food; *buckram bag* the lawyer's docu-
   ment case, made of buckram
34, 36 *stop* fill up a cavity in
35 *pellitory of Spain* a plant with a hot taste, like ginger or peppermint
38 *pudding-pie* baked meat pie

Which we clerks find great relief in.

WINIFRED   I shall have no stomach.

SANITONELLA

No matter and you have not, I may pleasure   40
Some of our learned counsel with 't; I have done it
Many a time and often, when a cause
Has proved like an after-game at Irish.

Enter CRISPIANO *like a Judge, with another* JUDGE; CONTILUPO,
and another LAWYER *at one bar;* ROMELIO, ARIOSTO, *at another;*
          LEONORA *with a black veil over her, and* JULIO

CRISPIANO

'Tis a strange suit: is Leonora come?

CONTILUPO

She's here my lord; make way there for the lady.   45

CRISPIANO

Take off her veil: it seems she is ashamed
To look her cause i'th' face.

CONTILUPO   She's sick, my lord.

ARIOSTO

She's mad, my lord, and would be kept more dark.
[*To* ROMELIO] By your favour sir, I have now occasion
To be at your elbow, and within this half hour   50
Shall entreat you to be angry, very angry.

CRISPIANO

Is Romelio come?

ROMELIO

I am here my lord, and called, I do protest,
To answer what I know not, for as yet
I am wholly ignorant of what the court   55
Will charge me with.

CRISPIANO   I assure you, the proceeding
Is most unequal then, for I perceive

---

39 *stomach* appetite
44 *suit:* ed. (Suite, Q; suit. – Dyce; suit. Hazlitt; Suite – Lucas);
   come? Dyce, Hazlitt (come. Q, Lucas)
48 *more dark* in greater darkness: in the 16th and 17th centuries
   lunatics were kept in the dark

---

43 *an after-game at Irish* Irish was similar to backgammon. In a second,
   or after-game, the loser of the first game would try to win. The implica-
   tion here, confirmed by Lucas's comment on the passage (II, 350), is
   that such games were tedious; but Dent (p. 310) cites instances of the
   after-game being considered proverbially short.

The counsel of the adverse party furnished
With full instruction.

ROMELIO

Pray my lord, who is my accuser?

CRISPIANO   'Tis your mother.   60

ROMELIO [aside]

She has discovered Contarino's murder:
If she prove so unnatural, to call
My life in question, I am armed to suffer
This to end all my losses.

CRISPIANO   Sir, we will do you
This favour: you shall hear the accusation,   65
Which being known, we will adjourn the court
Till a fortnight hence; you may provide your counsel.

ARIOSTO

I advise you, take their proffer,
Or else the lunacy runs in a blood,
You are more mad than she.

ROMELIO   What are you sir?   70

ARIOSTO

An angry fellow that would do thee good,
For goodness' sake itself, I do protest,
Neither for love nor money.

ROMELIO

Prithee stand further, I shall gall your gout else.

ARIOSTO

Come, come, I know you for an East Indy merchant,   75
You have a spice of pride in you still.

ROMELIO

My lord, I am so strengthened in my innocence,
For any the least shadow of a crime,
Committed 'gainst my mother, or the world,
That she can charge me with, here do I make it   80
My humble suit, only this hour and place
May give it as full hearing, and as free
And unrestrained a sentence.

CRISPIANO   Be not too confident;
You have cause to fear.

ROMELIO   Let fear dwell with earthquakes,

61 *discovered* made known
62–3 *to call/My life in question* to charge me with an offence
   punishable by death
69 *runs in a blood* runs in the family

Shipwracks at sea, or prodigies in heaven;   85
I cannot set myself so many fathom
Beneath the height of my true heart, as fear.

ARIOSTO
Very fine words, I assure you, if they were
To any purpose.

CRISPIANO   Well, have your entreaty:
And if your own credulity undo you,   90
Blame not the court hereafter. [*To* CONTILUPO] Fall to your
plea.

CONTILUPO
May it please your lordship and the reverend court
To give me leave to open to you a case
So rare, so altogether void of precedent
That I do challenge all the spacious volumes   95
Of the whole civil law to show the like.
We are of counsel for this gentlewoman,
We have received our fee, yet the whole course
Of what we are to speak, is quite against her;
Yet we'll deserve our fee too. There stands one,   100
Romelio the merchant; I will name him to you
Without either title or addition:
For those false beams of his supposed honour,
As void of true heat, as are all painted fires
Or glow-worms in the dark, suit him all basely   105
As if he had bought his gentry from the herald
With money got by extortion: I will first
Produce this Æsop's crow, as he stands forfeit
For the long use of his gay borrowed plumes,
And then let him hop naked. I come to th' point.   110
'T 'as been a dream in Naples, very near

---

85 *prodigies in heaven* comets, considered to be portents of disaster
87 *as fear* as to fear
104 *all painted* Q (painted Dyce)

104-5 Dent points out a parallel with *Pericles*, II. iii, 43–4:
     . . . his son's like a glow-worm in the night,
     The which hath fire in darkness, none in light.
    A similar image is found in *The White Devil*, V. i, 40–1 and is repeated
    in *The Duchess of Malfi*, IV. ii, 141–2.
108 *Æsop's crow* Lucas recalls that it was actually a jackdaw who, in Æsop's
    fable, decked himself in borrowed plumes. But Robert Greene shares
    the error when he refers to Shakespeare as 'an upstart crow, beautified
    with our feathers' (*Groats-worth of Witte*, 1592).

This eight and thirty years, that this Romelio
Was nobly descended; he has ranked himself
With the nobility, shamefully usurped
Their place, and in a kind of saucy pride,   115
Which, like to mushrooms, ever grow most rank
When they do spring from dunghills, sought to o'ersway
The Fieschi, the Grimaldi, Doria
And all the ancient pillars of our state;
View now what he is come to: this poor thing   120
Without a name, this cuckoo hatched i'th' nest
Of a hedge-sparrow.

ROMELIO
Speaks he all this to me?

ARIOSTO   Only to you sir.

ROMELIO
I do not ask thee; prithee, hold thy prating.

ARIOSTO
Why very good, you will be presently   125
As angry as I could wish.

CONTILUPO
What title shall I set to this base coin?
He has no name, and for's aspect, he seems
A giant in a May-game, that within
Is nothing but a porter. I'll undertake,   130
He had as good have travelled all his life
With gipsies: I will sell him to any man
For an hundred chequeens, and he that buys him of me,

129 *A giant in a May-game* 'Jack in the Green, a giant figure, probably
     in origin a vegetation-spirit, was a central figure of May-Day
     celebrations' (Gunby)
133 *chequeens* also called zecchins, were gold coins used in Italy and
     Turkey

116–17 Cf. *The White Devil*, III. iii, 46–8. The use of the mushroom image
        to refer to social upstarts was proverbial (Tilley, M 1319), but Dent
        asserts that the placing of the mushroom on a dunghill appears to have
        been original to Webster.
118   The three families named here belonged to Genoa, not Naples. They
        were the centre of a dispute concerning the quality of their nobility
        in the late 16th century. Dent suggests (p. 311) that a reference to the
        John Flisco who was chosen Duke of Genoa in the mid-16th century in
        the paragraph preceding the one which formed his source for ll. 113-19
        may have led to his writing 'Fliski' instead of 'Fieschi' (see Textual
        Appendix A).

Shall lose by th' hand too.

ARIOSTO   Lo, what you are come to:
You that did scorn to trade in any thing   135
But gold or spices, or your cochineal!
He rates you now at poor John.

ROMELIO   Out upon thee,
I would thou wert of his side –

ARIOSTO   Would you so?

ROMELIO
The devil and thee together on each hand,
To prompt the lawyer's memory when he founders.   140

CRISPIANO
Signior Contilupo, the court holds it fit,
You leave this stale declaiming 'gainst the person,
And come to the matter.

CONTILUPO   Now I shall, my lord.

CRISPIANO
It shows a poor malicious eloquence,
And it is strange, men of your gravity   145
Will not forgo it: verily, I presume,
If you but heard yourself speaking with my ears,
Your phrase would be more modest.

CONTILUPO   Good my lord, be assured,
I will leave all circumstance, and come to th' purpose:
This Romelio is a bastard.

ROMELIO   How, a bastard!   150
Oh mother, now the day begins grow hot
On your side.

CONTILUPO   Why, she is your accuser.

ROMELIO
I had forgot that; was my father married
To any other woman, at the time
Of my begetting?

CONTILUPO   That's not the business.   155

ROMELIO
I turn me then to you that were my mother,
But by what name I am to call you now,
You must instruct me: were you ever married
To my father?

134 *by th' hand* by the deal
136 *cochineal* red dye derived from the female of the insect *coccus
   cacti*; it was also used medicinally
137 *poor John* dried and salted coarse fish, usually hake
138 *side* – ed. (side, Q)

LEONORA   To my shame I speak it, never.
CRISPIANO
  Not to Francisco Romelio?
LEONORA   May it please your lordships,   160
  To him I was, but he was not his father.
CONTILUPO
  Good my lord, give us leave in a few words,
  To expound the riddle, and to make it plain,
  Without the least of scruple: for I take it,
  There cannot be more lawful proof i'th' world,   165
  Than the oath of the mother.
CRISPIANO   Well then, to your proofs,
  And be not tedious.
CONTILUPO   I'll conclude in a word.
  Some nine-and thirty years since, which was the time
  This woman was married, Francisco Romelio,
  This gentleman's putative father and her husband,   170
  Being not married to her past a fortnight,
  Would needs go travel; did so, and continued
  In France and the Low Countries eleven months:
  Take special note o'th' time, I beseech your lordship,
  For it makes much to th' business. In his absence   175
  He left behind to sojourn at his house
  A Spanish gentleman, a fine spruce youth
  By the lady's confession, and you may be sure
  He was no eunuch neither: he was one
  Romelio loved very dearly, as oft haps   180
  No man alive more welcome to the husband
  Than he that makes him cuckold.
  This gentleman, I say,
  Breaking all laws of hospitality
  Got his friend's wife with child, a full two months   185
  Fore the husband returned.
SANITONELLA [aside]   Good sir, forget not the lambskin.
CONTILUPO [aside]
  I warrant thee.
SANITONELLA [aside] I will pinch by the buttock
  To put you in mind of't.
CONTILUPO [aside]   Prithee, hold thy prating.
  What's to be practised now, my lord? Marry this:
  Romelio being a young novice, not acquainted   190
  With this precedence, very innocently

164 *scruple* doubt
5 * *

Returning home from travel, finds his wife
Grown an excellent good huswife, for she had set
Her women to spin flax, and to that use
Had in a study which was built of stone,   195
Stored up at least an hundredweight of flax:
Marry, such a thread as was to be spun from the flax,
I think the like was never heard of.

CRISPIANO   What was that?
CONTILUPO
You may be certain, she would lose no time,
In bragging that her husband had got up   200
Her belly: to be short, at seven months' end,
Which was the time of her delivery,
And when she felt herself to fall in travail
She makes her waiting woman, as by mischance,
Set fire to the flax, the fright whereof   205
As they pretend, causes this gentlewoman
To fall in pain, and be delivered
Eight weeks afore her reckoning.

SANITONELLA [aside]
Now sir, remember the lambskin.

CONTILUPO
The midwife straight howls out, there was no hope   210
Of th' infant's life, swaddles it in a flayed lambskin,
As a bird hatched too early, makes it up
With three-quarters of a face, that made it look
Like a changeling, cries out to Romelio
To have it christened, lest it should depart   215
Without that it came for: and thus are many served
That take care to get gossips for those children,
To which they might be godfathers themselves,
And yet be no arch-puritans neither.

193 *huswife* (pronounced 'huzziv') housewife: (i) a woman who
manages her home thriftily; (ii) a loose woman, hussy
195 *study* private room
212–13 *makes ... face* bundles it up so that it appears only to have
three-quarters of a face
214 *changeling* an ugly or mentally deficient child supposed to have
been left by the fairies in place of a normal child
216 *Without that it came for* i.e., salvation
217 *gossips* godparents

217–19 At one time members of the Church of England were not allowed to
become godparents to their own children. Puritans believed that parents
only should be responsible for a child's spiritual education.

CRISPIANO   No more!

ARIOSTO

Pray my lord, give him way, you spoil his oratory else: 220
Thus would they jest were they fee'd to open
Their sisters' cases.

CRISPIANO   You have urged enough;
You first affirm, her husband was away from her
Eleven months?

CONTILUPO   Yes my lord.

CRISPIANO

And at seven months' end,   225
After his return, she was delivered
Of this Romelio, and had gone her full time?

CONTILUPO

True my lord.

CRISPIANO

So by this account this gentleman was begot
In his supposed father's absence?

CONTILUPO   You have it fully.   230

CRISPIANO

A most strange suit this: 'tis beyond example,
Either time past, or present, for a woman
To publish her own dishonour voluntarily,
Without being called in question, some forty years
After the sin committed, and her counsel   235
To enlarge the offence with as much oratory,
As ever I did hear them in my life
Defend a guilty woman; 'tis most strange:
Or why with such a poisoned violence
Should she labour her son's undoing? We observe   240
Obedience of creatures to the law of nature
Is the stay of the whole world: here that law is broke,

232 *time past, or present* in time past, or present
238 *Defend . . . woman* defend a guilty woman with

241–2 This appears to be taken directly from the conclusion of the most
    famous passage of Hooker's *Ecclesiastical Polity*, Book I; but, since
    Webster has no other borrowings from Hooker, Dent suggests (p. 312)
    that Webster's indebtedness here may have been at second hand.

For though our civil law makes difference
'Tween the base and the legitimate, compassionate nature
Makes them equal; nay, she many times prefers them.   245
I pray resolve me sir, have not you and your mother
Had some suit in law together lately?

ROMELIO
None my lord.

CRISPIANO
No? No contention about parting your goods?

ROMELIO
Not any.

CRISPIANO No flaw, no unkindness?   250

ROMELIO
None that ever arrived at my knowledge.

CRISPIANO
Bethink yourself, this cannot choose but savour
Of a woman's malice deeply; and I fear,
Y'are practised upon most devilishly. How happed
Gentlewoman, you revealed this no sooner?   255

LEONORA
While my husband lived, my lord, I durst not.

CRISPIANO
I should rather ask you, why you reveal it now?

LEONORA
Because, my lord, I loathed that such a sin
Should lie smothered with me in my grave; my penitence,
Though to my shame, prefers the revealing of it   260

---

250 *flaw* storm, squall; imperfection: cf. *The White Devil*, I. ii, 56–7
254 *happed* how did it happen?

243–5 Cf. *The Duchess of Malfi*, IV. i, 36–8:
> For though our national law distinguish bastards
> From true legitimate issue, compassionate nature
> Makes them all equal.

Dent (p. 229) finds two sources here most interestingly combined. From Pierre Matthieu's supplement to Jean de Serres's *General Inventorie of the History of France*, translated by Edward Grimeston, comes the idea: 'although the Law doth distinguish Bastards from them that are lawfully begotten, yet nature makes no difference'; from Antonio de Guevara's *Diall of Princes*, translated by Sir Thomas North, comes the language of its expression in *The Devil's Law-Case*: 'And admit that in this life, fortune doth make difference betwene us in estates, yet nature in time of our birth, and death, dothe make us all equall'.

'Bove worldly reputation.
CRISPIANO   Your penitence?
Might not your penitence have been as hearty,
Though it had never summoned to the court
Such a conflux of people?
LEONORA
Indeed I might have confessed it, privately   265
To th' church, I grant; but you know repentance
Is nothing without satisfaction.
CRISPIANO
Satisfaction? Why, your husband's dead;
What satisfaction can you make him?
LEONORA
The greatest satisfaction in the world, my lord,   270
To restore the land to th'right heir, and that's
My daughter.
CRISPIANO   Oh she's straight begot then.
ARIOSTO
Very well: may it please this honourable court,
If he be a bastard, and must forfeit his land for't,
She has proved herself a strumpet, and must lose   275
Her dower; let them go a-begging together.
SANITONELLA
Who shall pay us our fees then?
CRISPIANO
Most just.
ARIOSTO   You may see now what an old house
You are like to pull over your head, dame.
ROMELIO
Could I conceive this publication   280
Grew from a hearty penitence, I could bear
My undoing the more patiently; but my lord,
There is no reason, as you said even now,
To satisfy me: but this suit of hers
Springs from a devilish malice, and her pretence   285
Of a grieved conscience, and religion,
Like to the horrid powder-treason in England,
Has a most bloody unnatural revenge

275–6 Lucas, II, 353, notes that, according to English law, Leonora would
    have had to forfeit her dowry only if she had lived with her lover.
287 *the horrid powder-treason in England* Thomas Percy, one of the con-
    spirators involved in the Gunpowder Plot of 1605, did nurse a personal
    grudge against James I: see Lucas, II, 353–4.

Hid under it. Oh the violencies of women!
Why, they are creatures made up and compounded   290
Of all monsters, poisoned minerals,
And sorcerous herbs that grows.

ARIOSTO   Are you angry yet?

ROMELIO
Would man express a bad one, let him forsake
All natural example, and compare
One to another; they have no more mercy   295
Than ruinous fires in great tempests.

ARIOSTO
Take heed you do not crack your voice, sir.

ROMELIO
Hard-hearted creatures, good for nothing else,
But to wind dead bodies.

ARIOSTO   Yes, to weave seaming lace
With the bones of their husbands that were long since
    buried,   300
And curse them when they tangle.

ROMELIO   Yet why do I
Take bastardy so distastefully, when i'th' world,
A many things that are essential parts
Of greatness, are but by-slips, and are fathered
On the wrong parties;   305
Preferment in the world a many times,
Basely begotten? Nay, I have observed
The immaculate justice of a poor man's cause,
In such a court as this, has not known whom
To call father, which way to direct itself   310
For compassion: but I forget my temper, –
Only that I may stop that lawyer's throat,
I do beseech the court, and the whole world,
They will not think the baselier of me,

291 *poisoned* poisonous   291–2 cf. *The White Devil*, I. ii, 263–4
293 *man* ed. (men Q)
299 *wind* i.e., in a winding sheet, or shroud; *seaming lace* lace to cover
    seams
300 *bones* small bones were used as bobbins in lace weaving
304 *by-slips* bastards
311 *temper,* – ed. (temper, Q; temper: Dyce, Hazlitt; temper – Lucas)

For the vice of a mother: for that woman's sin,   315
To which you all dare sware when it was done,
I would not give my consent.
CRISPIANO   Stay, here's an accusation,
But here's no proof: what was the Spaniard's name
You accuse of adultery?
CONTILUPO   Don Crispiano, my lord.
CRISPIANO
. What part of Spain was he born in?
CONTILUPO   In Castile.   320
JULIO [aside]
This may prove my father.
SANITONELLA   And my master;
My client's spoiled then.
CRISPIANO
I knew that Spaniard well: if you be a bastard,
Such a man being your father, I dare vouch you
A gentleman; and in that, Signior Contilupo,   325
Your oratory went a little too far.
When do we name Don John of Austria,
The emperor's son, but with reverence?
And I have known in divers families,
The bastards the greater spirits; but to th' purpose: 330
What time was this gentleman begot? And be sure
You lay your time right.
ARIOSTO   Now the metal comes
To the touchstone.
CONTILUPO   In anno seventy-one, my lord.

---

315 *for that* as for that
322 *spoiled* ruined

315–17 *for that . . . my consent.* Dent (p. 312) suggests that Webster may
here be indebted to the analogous wit in Machiavelli's *Florentine History*,
the Earl Francesco who, when called a bastard, replied that 'he knew
not in what sort Sforza his father, had used his mother Maddonna
Lucia, because he was not there present. So as of that which was done
by them he could receive neither blame nor commendation'.

321 *And my master* 'how could this statement of Contilupo's come as a
surprise to Sanitonella, when he had himself drawn up the brief which
is Contilupo's sole source of information?' (Lucas, II, 354)

327 *Don John of Austria* an illegitimate son of the emperor who, as Charles
V, ruled the Holy Roman Empire and, as Charles I, ruled Spain. Don
John was acknowledged by his father in a codicil to his will and officially
recognized by Philip II, his father's successor in Spain, in 1559, the
year after his father's death. Cf. IV. ii, 334n.

CRISPIANO
Very well, seventy-one: the battle of Lepanto
Was fought in't, a most remarkable time, 335
'Twill lie for no man's pleasure: and what proof is there
More than the affirmation of the mother,
Of this corporal dealing?
CONTILUPO The deposition
Of a waiting-woman served her the same time.
CRISPIANO
Where is she?
CONTILUPO Where is our solicitor 340
With the waiting-woman?
ARIOSTO Room for the bag and baggage!
SANITONELLA
Here my lord, *ore tenus*.
CRISPIANO And what can you say, gentlewoman?
WINIFRED
Please your lordship, I was the party that dealt in the
business, and brought them together.
CRISPIANO
Well. 345
WINIFRED
And conveyed letters between them.
CRISPIANO
What needed letters, when 'tis said he lodged in her house?
WINIFRED
A running ballad now and then to her viol, for he was never
well, but when he was fiddling.

338 *deposition* statement given as evidence, usually written
339 *served* that served
341 *bag and baggage* i.e., the lawyer, with his buckram bag, and
Winifred
342 *ore tenus* 'by word of mouth': either Winifred is to be examined
without a written deposition or the phrase means that she is here
in person—see Lucas, II, 355
348 *running* lightly tripping; *to her viol* set to the music of her viol
349 *fiddling* a *double-entendre*

334 *the battle of Lepanto* i.e., the battle at which the forces of the Christian
League, under Don John of Austria, defeated the Turks, on 7 October
1571. It was the last great sea battle in which both sides used oar-pro-
pelled ships. It was also remarkable for the enormous number of
casualties on both sides.

CRISPIANO

Speak to the purpose: did you ever know them in bed   350
together?

WINIFRED

No my lord, but I have brought him to the bed-side.

CRISPIANO

That was somewhat near to the business; and what, did you
help him off with his shoes?

WINIFRED

He wore no shoes, an't please you my lord.   355

CRISPIANO

No? what then, pumps?

WINIFRED

Neither.

CRISPIANO

Boots were not fit for his journey.

WINIFRED

He wore tennis-court woollen slippers, for fear of creak-
ing, sir, and making a noise, to wake the rest o'th' house.   360

CRISPIANO

Well, and what did he there, in his tennis-court woollen
slippers?

WINIFRED

Please your lordship, question me in Latin, for the cause
is very foul; the examiner o'th' court was fain to get it out of
me alone i'th' counting-house, 'cause he would not spoil   365
the youth o' th' office.

ARIOSTO

Here's a Latin spoon, and a long one, to feed with the devil.

WINIFRED

I'd be loth to be ignorant that way, for I hope to marry a

---

356 *pumps* light indoor shoes without fastening, kept on by their
tight fit
365 *spoil* have a detrimental effect upon
368 *that way* i.e., of Latin; of how to sup with the devil

---

367 *Latin* usual meaning; brass: Dyce and Lucas recall a story of Shakespeare using the same pun when puzzled as to what to present to his
godson, Ben Jonson's child, as a gift: 'I' faith *Ben*: I'le e'en give him a
dozen good Lattin spoones, and thou shalt translate them'. There is
also an allusion here to the proverbial need of a long spoon for supping
with the devil.

proctor, and take my pleasure abroad at the commencements
with him.   370

ARIOSTO
Come closer to the business.

WINIFRED
I will come as close as modesty will give me leave. Truth is,
every morning when he lay with her, I made a caudle for him,
by the appointment of my mistress, which he would still
refuse, and call for small drink.   375

CRISPIANO
Small drink?

ARIOSTO
For a julep.

WINIFRED
And said he was wondrous thirsty.

CRISPIANO
What's this to the purpose?

WINIFRED
Most effectual, my lord: I have heard them laugh together   380
extremely, and the curtain rods fall from the tester of the bed,
and he ne'er came from her, but he thrust money in my
hand; and once, in truth, he would have had some dealing
with me; which I took, he thought 'twould be the only way
i'th' world to make me keep counsel the better.   385

SANITONELLA [aside]
That's a stinger; 'tis a good wench, be not daunted.

CRISPIANO
Did you ever find the print of two in the bed?

---

369 *proctor* the equivalent, in courts administering civil or canon law,
   of a solicitor in courts of equity or common law; *abroad* i.e., in
   the city, not necessarily out of the country
369 *commencements* beginnings of law-terms
373 *caudle* a strengthening beverage of gruel mixed with wine, or sugar
   and spices
374 *still* always
375 *small drink* drink with little or no alcoholic content
381 *tester* canopy
382–3 *my hand;* Q, Lucas (my hand, – Dyce; my Hand, Hazlitt)
384 *me; which I took, he* ed.: see Textual Appendix A

---

377 *a julep* a soothing drink. As such drinks could form the basis of soothing
   medicine, Ariosto here implies that, if the Spaniard refused something
   which would strengthen his desire, he must have wished to diminish
   it (Lucas, II, 355).

WINIFRED

What a question's that to be asked! May it please your
lordship, 'tis to be thought he lay nearer to her than so.

CRISPIANO

What age are you of, gentlewoman?   390

WINIFRED

About six and forty, my lord.

CRISPIANO   Anno seventy-one,

And Romelio is thirty-eight: by that reckoning,
You were a bawd at eight year old: now verily,
You fell to the trade betimes.

SANITONELLA   There y'are from the bias.

WINIFRED

I do not know my age directly; sure I am elder: I can   395
remember two great frosts, and three great plagues, and the
loss of Calais, and the first coming up of the breeches with the
great codpiece. And I pray what age do you take me of then?

SANITONELLA [aside]

Well come off again!

ARIOSTO

An old hunted hare, she has all her doubles.   400

ROMELIO

For your own gravities,
And the reverence of the court, I do beseech you,
Rip up the cause no further, but proceed
To sentence.

CRISPIANO   One question more and I have done:

Might not this Crispiano, this Spaniard,   405
Lie with your mistress at some other time,

388 *asked!* Dyce, Hazlitt (askt. Q; askt! Lucas)
394 *betimes* early; *from the bias* off-course: in bowling the bias was the
     set course of the bowl
397 *coming up* coming into fashion; also a *double-entendre*
400 *doubles* evasive turns in argument—from the turns a hare makes to
     deceive the following hounds

395–8 In response to Crispiano's calculation that, if she is only forty-six,
she must have been an eight-year-old bawd, Winifred pretends to
remember events in the past which will establish her as much older.
Each one she mentions increases her age, as the *two great frosts* were
those of 1607–08 and 1564; the *three great plagues* were probably those
of 1603, 1592–94, and 1563; *the loss of Calais* by the English to the Duke
of Guise took place in January 1558; *breeches with the great codpiece*
became fashionable in the reign of Henry VIII, *c.* 1515.

Either afore or after, than i'th' absence
Of her husband?
LEONORA   Never.
CRISPIANO   Are you certain of that?
LEONORA
On my soul, never.
CRISPIANO   That's well; he never lay with her,
But in anno seventy-one, let that be remembered.   410
Stand you aside a while. Mistress, the truth is,
I knew this Crispiano, lived in Naples
At the same time, and loved the gentleman
As my bosom friend; and as I do remember,
The gentleman did leave his picture with you,   415
If age or neglect have not in so long time ruined it.
LEONORA
I preserve it still my lord.
CRISPIANO   I pray let me see't,
Let me see the face I then loved so much to look on.
LEONORA
Fetch it.
WINIFRED   I shall, my lord.
CRISPIANO   No, no gentlewoman,
I have other business for you. [*Exit one for the picture*]   420
FIRST SURGEON [*aside*]
Now were the time to cut Romelio's throat.
And accuse him for your murder.
CONTARINO [*aside*]   By no means.
SECOND SURGEON [*aside*]
Will you not let us be men of fashion,
And down with him now he's going?
CONTARINO
Peace, let's attend the sequel.
CRISPIANO   I commend you lady,   425
There was a main matter of conscience:
How many ills spring from adultery!
First, the supreme law is violated,
Nobility oft stained with bastardy,
Inheritance of land falsely possessed,   430
The husband scorned, wife shamed, and babes unblessed.

[*Enter one with*] the picture

So, hang it up i'th' court: you have heard
What has been urged against Romelio.

431 s.d.: *The Picture* opposite l. 432 in Q

Now, my definitive sentence in this cause
Is, I will give no sentence at all.
ARIOSTO   No?   435
CRISPIANO
No, I cannot, for I am made a party.
SANITONELLA [*aside*]
How, a party? Here are fine cross tricks;
What the devil will he do now?
CRISPIANO
Signior Ariosto, His Majesty of Spain
Confers my place upon you by this patent,   440
Which till this urgent hour I have kept
From your knowledge: may you thrive in't, noble sir,
And do that which but few in our place do,
Go to their grave uncursed.
ARIOSTO   This law business
Will leave me so small leisure to serve God,   445
I shall serve the king the worse.
SANITONELLA [*aside*]   Is he a judge?
We must then look for all conscience, and no law;
He'll beggar all his followers.
CRISPIANO [*to* ROMELIO]
Sir, I am of your counsel, for the cause in hand
Was begun at such a time, 'fore you could speak;   450
You had need therefore have one speak for you.
ARIOSTO
Stay, I do here first make protestation,
I ne'er took fee of this Romelio,
For being of his counsel, which may free me,
Being now his judge, fro' the imputation   455
Of taking a bribe. Now sir, speak your mind.
CRISPIANO
I do first entreat, that the eyes of all here present
May be fixed upon this.

---

437 *cross tricks* ' "a fine red herring"—"cross tricks" being tricks cut
    irrelevantly across the progress of the main issue' (Lucas)
455 *fro*' Hazlitt (for Q, Dyce, Lucas)

---

437 *How, a party*! Lucas (II, 356) points out that this is another incon-
    sistency in the characterization of Sanitonella (cf. IV. ii, 321). Perhaps
    he had not recognized Crispiano as the judge.
444–6 Cf. Wolsey's statement in *Henry VIII*, III. ii, 455–7:
        Had I but serv'd my God with half the zeal
        I serv'd my king, he would not in mine age
        Have left me naked to mine enemies.   (Lucas, II, 357)

LEONORA
  Oh, I am confounded: this is Crispiano!
JULIO [*aside*]
  This is my father; how the judges have bleared him!   460
WINIFRED [*aside*]
  You may see the truth will out in spite of the devil.
CRISPIANO
  Behold, I am the shadow of this shadow;
  Age has made me so; take from me forty years,
  And I was such a summer fruit as this,
  At least the painter feigned so: for indeed,   465
  Painting and epitaphs are both alike,
  They flatter us, and say we have been thus.
  But I am the party here, that stands accused
  For adultery with this woman, in the year
  Seventy-one: now I call you, my lord, to witness,   470
  Four years before that time I went to th'Indies,
  And till this month, did never set my foot since
  In Europe; and for any former incontinence,
  She has vowed there was never any: what remains then,
  But this is a mere practice 'gainst her son,   475
  And I beseech the court it may be sifted,
  And most severely punished.
SANITONELLA [*aside*]   Ud's foot, we are spoiled;
  Why, my client's proved an honest woman!
WINIFRED [*aside*]
  What do you think will become of me now?
SANITONELLA [*aside*]
  You'll be made dance *Lachrimæ*, I fear,   480
  At a cart's tail.
ARIOSTO   You, mistress, where are you now?
  Your tennis-court slips, and your ta'en drink
  In a morning for your hot liver; where's the man
  Would have had some dealing with you, that you might

460 *bleared him!* ed. thrown dust in his eyes: see Textual Appendix A
478 *honest* chaste
480 *Lachrimæ* 'Lachrimæ (Tears) was a set of seven pavanes written
     by John Dowland in 1608' (Gunby)
481 *At a cart's tail* i.e., as she is whipped for being a bawd
482 *slips* Q. Lucas commented on his emendation 'slip[per]s': 'I can
     find no authority of *slips* = "slippers"; but of course Q *may* be
     right'
483 *your hot liver* i.e., the hot liver [Crispiano's] you were talking
     about; the liver was supposed to be the seat of sensual passion

Keep counsel the better?   485

WINIFRED
May it please the court, I am but a young thing, and was
drawn arsy-varsy into the business.

ARIOSTO
How young? Of five-and-forty?

WINIFRED
Five-and-forty! And shall please you, I am not five-and-
twenty: she made me colour my hair with bean-flour, to seem   490
elder than I was; and then my rotten teeth, with eating
sweet-meats: – why, should a farrier look in my mouth, he
might mistake my age. Oh mistress, mistress, you are an
honest woman, and you may be ashamed on't, to abuse the
court thus.   495

LEONORA
Whatsoe'er I have attempted,
'Gainst my own fame, or the reputation
Of that gentleman my son, the Lord Contarino
Was the cause of it.

CONTARINO [aside]   Who, I?

ARIOSTO
He that should have married your daughter?   500
It was a plot belike, then, to confer
The land on her that should have been his wife.

LEONORA
More than I have said already, all the world
Shall ne'er extract from me; I entreat from both
Your equal pardons.

JULIO   And I from you, sir.   505

CRISPIANO
Sirrah, stand you aside,
I will talk with you hereafter.

JULIO
I could never away with after-reckonings.

LEONORA
And now my lords, I do most voluntarily
Confine myself unto a stricter prison,   510

487 *arsy-varsy* backside foremost; willy-nilly
490 *bean-flour* ed. (bean-flower Q, Dyce, Hazlitt, Lucas). As bean-
flowers were violet-tinted, it is more likely that a bean powder
was used by Winifred. At this time *flower* and *flour* could mean
the same thing
494 *abuse* deceive
508 *away with* put up with; *after-reckonings* final accounts

And a severer penance than this court
Can impose: I am entered into religion.
CONTARINO [*aside*]
    I the cause of this practice! This ungodly woman
    Has sold herself to falsehood: I will now
    Reveal myself.
ERCOLE [*revealing himself*] Stay my lord, here's a window   515
    To let in more light to the court.
CONTARINO
    Mercy upon me! Oh, that thou art living,
    Is mercy indeed!
FIRST SURGEON [*aside*] Stay, keep in your shell
    A little longer!
ERCOLE   I am Ercole.
ARIOSTO
    A guard upon him for the death of Contarino!   520
ERCOLE
    I obey the arrest o' th' court.
ROMELIO
    Oh sir, you are happily restored to life,
    And to us your friends.
ERCOLE   Away, thou art the traitor
    I only live to challenge; this former suit
    Touched but thy fame; this accusation   525
    Reaches to thy fame and life: the brave Contarino
    In generally supposed slain by this hand,
CONTARINO [*aside*]
    How knows he the contrary?
ERCOLE   But truth is,
    Having received from me some certain wounds,
    Which were not mortal, this vild murderer   530
    Being by will deputed overseer
    Of the nobleman's estate, to his sister's use,
    That he might make him sure from surviving,
    To revoke that will, stole to him in's bed, and killed him.
ROMELIO
    Strange, unheard of! More practice yet!   535
ARIOSTO
    What proof of this?
ERCOLE
    The report of his mother delivered to me,

531 *overseer* executor
533 *sure from* Qb (sure Qa)
534 *in's* Q (in his Dyce)

In distraction for Contarino's death.

CONTARINO [*aside*]
For my death? I begin to apprehend
That the violence of this woman's love to me   540
Might practise this disinheriting of her son.

ARIOSTO
What say you to this Leonora?

LEONORA
Such a thing I did utter out of my distraction:
But how the court will censure that report,
I leave to their wisdoms.

ARIOSTO   My opinion is,   545
That this late slander urged against her son
Takes from her all manner of credit: she
That would not stick to deprive him of his living,
Will as little tender his life.

LEONORA   I beseech the court,
I may retire myself to my place of penance,   550
I have vowed myself and my woman.

ARIOSTO
Go when you please.   [*Exeunt* LEONORA *and* WINIFRED]
   [*to* ERCOLE] What should move you be thus forward
In the accusation?

ERCOLE   My love to Contarino.

ARIOSTO
Oh, it bore very bitter fruit at your last meeting.

ERCOLE
'Tis true: but I begun to love him,   555
When I had most cause to hate him; when our bloods
Embraced each other, then I pitied,
That so much valour should be hazarded
On the fortune of a single rapier,
And not spent against the Turk.

ARIOSTO   Stay sir, be well advised.   560
There is no testimony but your own
[*turning to* ROMELIO] To approve you slew him, therefore no
   other way
To decide it, but by duel.

---

562 s.d. Lucas

547–9 Cf. *The Duchess of Malfi*, V. i, 11–13:
   I cannot think they mean well to your life,
   That do deprive you of your means of life,
   Your living.

CONTARINO
Yes my lord, I dare affirm 'gainst all the world,
This nobleman speaks truth.   565
ARIOSTO
You will make yourself a party in the duel?
ROMELIO
Let him, I will fight with them both; sixteen of them.
ERCOLE
Sir, I do not know you.
CONTARINO   Yes, but you have forgot me,
You and I have sweat in the breach together
At Malta.
ERCOLE   Cry you mercy, I have known   570
Of your nation brave soldiers.
JULIO [aside]   Now if my father
Have any true spirit in him, I'll recover
His good opinion. [To CONTARINO] Do you hear? Do not
    swear sir,
For I dare swear, that you will swear a lie,
A very filthy, stinking, rotten lie: 575
And if the lawyers think not this sufficient,
I'll give the lie in the stomach –
That's somewhat deeper than the throat –
Both here, and all France over and over,
From Marseilles, or Bayonne, to Calais sands,   580
And there draw my sword upon thee, and new scour it
In the gravel of thy kidneys.
ARIOSTO   You the defendant
Charged with the murder, and you second there,

571 *Of your nation* Contarino is disguised as a Dane. Lucas suggests (II,
    357) that this may have been intended by the actors, Queen Anne's
    Servants, as a tribute to her, since she was Danish. It would follow, if
    this were the case, that the play was performed before her death in
    1619.
578 *deeper than the throat* lying in one's throat was supposed to be lying that
    emanated from a more deep-seated mendacity than usual: cf. *Hamlet*,
    II. ii, 601–2.
580 *Calais sands* Enmity between English and Scottish courtiers led to
    frequent street duelling in the early years of the reign of James I, who
    therefore proscribed it in Proclamations of 1613 and 1614. In 1616 the
    carrying of pistols and daggers was forbidden. Thereafter, gentlemen
    wishing to fight a duel resorted to Calais sands or some other nearby
    continental duelling-ground.
581–2 Julio puns on the usual sense of *gravel* and the medical sense of stones
    in the kidneys.

Must be committed to the custody
Of the Knight-Marshal; and the court gives charge,   585
They be tomorrow ready in the lists
Before the sun be risen.

ROMELIO
I do entreat the court there be a guard
Placed o'er my sister, that she enter not
Into religion: she's rich my lords,   590
And the persuasions of friars, to gain
All her possessions to their monasteries,
May do much upon her.

ARIOSTO   We'll take order for her.

CRISPIANO
There's a nun too you have got with child,
How will you dispose of her?   595

ROMELIO
You question me, as if I were graved already;
When I have quenched this wild-fire in Ercole's
Tame blood, I'll tell you.   *Exit*

ERCOLE   You have judged today
A most confused practice, that takes end
In as bloody a trial, and we may observe   600
By these great persons, and their indirect
Proceedings, shadowed in a veil of state,
Mountains are deformed heaps, swelled up aloft;
Vales wholesomer, though lower, and trod on oft.

SANITONELLA
Well, I will put up my papers,   605
And send them to France for a precedent,
That they may not say yet, but for one strange law-suit,
We come somewhat near them.   *Exeunt*

Explicit Actus Quartus

---

585 *Knight-Marshal* an officer of the English royal household whose
     jurisdiction extended for a distance of 12 miles round the court
586 *lists* the places appointed for tournaments or duels
597 *wild-fire* furious and destructive fire, easily ignited and difficult
     to extinguish

603–4 these lines have been condensed from Sir William Alexander's
     Alexandrean Tragedy (1607), V, iii, lines 3362–5 (Dent, p. 313).

Actus Quintus, Scena Prima

Enter JOLENTA, *and* ANGIOLELLA *great-bellied*

JOLENTA

How dost thou friend? Welcome: thou and I
Were playfellows together, little children,
So small a while ago, that I presume,
We are neither of us wise yet.

ANGIOLELLA   A most sad truth
On my part.

JOLENTA   Why do you pluck your veil   5
Over your face?

ANGIOLELLA   If you will believe truth,
There's nought more terrible to a guilty heart,
Than the eye of a respected friend.

JOLENTA   Say friend,
Are you quick with child?

ANGIOLELLA

Too sure.

JOLENTA   How could you know   10
Of your first child: when you quickened?

ANGIOLELLA

How could you know, friend?
'Tis reported you are in the same taking.

JOLENTA

Ha, ha, ha! So 'tis given out:
But Ercole's coming to life again has shrunk   15
And made invisible my great belly; yes, faith,

---

8 *Than* ed. (As Q)

This scene takes place in the convent to which Angiolella belongs. Lucas
comments that there would be many alternative ways of staging this and
the following three scenes.

7–8 Lucas found the source of these lines in *Arcadia*, I, xiii: 'there is
nothing more terrible to a guilty hart, then the eie of a respected
friend'.

11 *Of your first child:* ed. (Of your first child Q; first/ Of your child Dyce;
[First of your] child Lucas; Of your first child, Hazlitt). Dyce's re-
arrangement of the words, accepted by Lucas, does not make very good
sense as it implies that Jolenta wonders how Angiolella didn't know she
was pregnant until she felt life. Q's wording, as it stands, but with a
colon added, I take to mean that Jolenta is so ignorant of matronly
matters that she is uncertain whether quickening is the first sign of
pregnancy.

My being with child was merely in supposition,
Not practice.

ANGIOLELLA   You are happy; what would I give
To be a maid again!

JOLENTA   Would you? To what purpose?
I would never give great purchase for that thing   20
Is in danger every hour to be lost: pray thee laugh.
A boy or a girl, for a wager?

ANGIOLELLA   What heaven please.

JOLENTA
Nay, nay, will you venture
A chain of pearl with me, whether?

ANGIOLELLA   I'll lay nothing;
I have ventured too much for't already, my fame.   25
I make no question, sister, you have heard
Of the intended combat?

JOLENTA   Oh what else?
I have a sweetheart in't, against a brother.

ANGIOLELLA
And I a dead friend, I fear; what good counsel
Can you minister unto me?

JOLENTA   Faith, only this,   30
Since there's no means i'th' world to hinder it,
Let thou and I wench get as far as we can
From the noise of it.

ANGIOLELLA   Whither?

JOLENTA   No matter, any whither.

ANGIOLELLA
Any whither, so you go not by sea:
I cannot abide rough water.   35

JOLENTA
Not endure to be tumbled? Say no more then,
We'll be land-soldiers for that trick: take heart,
Thy boy shall be born a brave Roman.

ANGIOLELLA   Oh, you mean
To go to Rome then.

JOLENTA   Within there!

[Enter a SERVANT]

Bear this letter

24 *whether* which, i.e., a boy or a girl
35 *rough* Qb (salt Qa)
36 *tumbled* a *double-entendre*
37 *for that trick* for that round of the (card) game

To the Lord Ercole. Now wench, I am for thee   40
All the world over.

ANGIOLELLA   I, like your shade, pursue you.

Exeunt

[Act V, Scene ii]

Enter PROSPERO *and* SANITONELLA

PROSPERO

Well, I do not think but to see you as pretty a piece of law-
flesh!

SANITONELLA

In time I may. Marry, I am resolved to take a new way for't.
You have lawyers take their clients' fees, and their backs are
no sooner turned, but they call them fools, and laugh at them.   5

PROSPERO

That's ill done of them.

SANITONELLA

There's one thing too that has a vild abuse in't.

PROSPERO

What's that?

SANITONELLA

Marry this: that no proctor in the term time be tolerated to
go to the tavern above six times i'th' forenoon.   10

PROSPERO

Why, man?

SANITONELLA

Oh sir, it makes their clients overtaken, and become friends
sooner than they would be.

Enter ERCOLE *with a letter, and* CONTARINO, *coming in friars'
habits, as having been at the Bathanites, a ceremony used afore
these combats*

ERCOLE

Leave the room, gentlemen.

[*Exeunt* PROSPERO *and* SANITONELLA]

41 *shade* shadow   3 *resolved* ed. (resolned Qa; resolued Qb)
12 *overtaken* overcome with drink

---

13 s.d. *Bathanites* Lucas (II, 358–9) suggested that this might be a corruption of Bethlemites. Of these at least three Orders have existed,
one of which was an order of knighthood founded by Pius II, and
similar to the Knights of St John of Jerusalem to which Ercole belonged.
There is, however, no evidence of any order prescribing a special
ceremony before judicial combats.

CONTARINO *speaks aside*
    Wherefore should I with such an obstinacy   15
    Conceal myself any longer? I am taught,
    That all the blood which will be shed tomorrow,
    Must fall upon my head; one question
    Shall fix it or untie it. [*To* ERCOLE] Noble brother,
    I would fain know how it is possible,   20
    When it appears you love the fair Jolenta
    With such a height of fervour, you were ready
    To father another's child, and marry her,
    You would so suddenly engage yourself
    To kill her brother, one that ever stood   25
    Your loyal and firm friend?
ERCOLE   Sir, I'll tell you:
    My love, as I have formerly protested,
    To Contarino, whose unfortunate end
    The traitor wrought; and here is one thing more,
    Deads all good thoughts of him, which I now received   30
    From Jolenta. [*He produces a letter*]
CONTARINO   In a letter?
ERCOLE   Yes, in this letter:
    For having sent to her to be resolved
    Most truly, who was father of the child,
    She writes back, that the shame she goes withal,
    Was begot by her brother.   35
CONTARINO
    Oh most incestuous villain!
ERCOLE   I protest,
    Before I thought 'twas Contarino's issue,
    And for that would have veiled her dishonour.
CONTARINO   No more.
    Has the armourer brought the weapons?
ERCOLE   Yes sir.
CONTARINO
    I will no more think of her.
ERCOLE   Of whom?   40
CONTARINO
    Of my mother – I was thinking of my mother.
    Call the armourer.   *Exeunt*

15 s.d.: Q reads *Con. speaks aside* in the margin, opposite ll. **16–17**
33 *letter?* ed. (Letter. Qa; Letter? Qb)

[Act V, Scene iii]

Enter [FIRST] SURGEON, *and* WINIFRED

WINIFRED
  You do love me sir, you say?
SURGEON   Oh most entirely.
WINIFRED
  And you will marry me?
SURGEON   Nay, I'll do more than that.
  The fashion of the world is many times
  To make a woman naught, and afterwards
  To marry her: but I, o'th' contrary,   5
  Will make you honest first, and afterwards
  Proceed to the wedlock
WINIFRED   Honest? What mean you by that?
SURGEON
  I mean, that your suborning the late law-suit
  Has got you a filthy report: now there's no way
  But to do some excellent piece of honesty,   10
  To recover your good name.
WINIFRED   How sir?
SURGEON
  You shall straight go, and reveal to your old mistress,
  For certain truth, Contarino is alive.
WINIFRED
  How, living?
SURGEON   Yes, he is living.
WINIFRED
  No, I must not tell her of it.
SURGEON   No, why?   15
WINIFRED
  For she did bind me yesterday by oath,
  Never more to speak of him.
SURGEON   You shall reveal it then
  To Ariosto the judge.
WINIFRED   By no means, he has heard me
  Tell so many lies i'th' court, he'll ne'er believe me.

1 s.d. [FIRST] SURGEON ed. (*Surgeon* Q): as it does not matter which
  of the surgeons takes part in this scene I have adhered to the
  speech-prefixes of Q
7 *Honest?* Q (Honest! Dyce, Hazlitt; Honest!–Lucas)

Dyce located this scene in Leonora's house; Lucas in the surgeon's.

What if I told it to the Capuchin?

SURGEON   You cannot   20
Think of a better; as for your young mistress
Who, as you told me, has persuaded you
To run away with her: let her have her humour.
I have a suit Romelio left i'th' house,
The habit of a Jew, that I'll put on,   25
And pretending I am robbed, by break of day,
Procure all passengers to be brought back,
And by the way reveal myself, and discover
The comical event. They say she's a little mad;
This will help to cure her: go, go presently,   30
And reveal it to the Capuchin.

WINIFRED   Sir, I shall.   *Exeunt*

[Act V, Scene iv]

Enter JULIO, PROSPERO, *and* SANITONELLA

JULIO
A pox on't,
I have undertaken the challenge very foolishly:
What if I do not appear to answer it?

PROSPERO
It would be absolute conviction
Of cowardice, and perjury: and the Dane   5
May to your public shame, reverse your arms,
Or have them ignominiously fastened
Under his horse-tail.

JULIO   I do not like that so well.
I see then I must fight whether I will or no.

PROSPERO
How does Romelio bear himself? They say,   10
He has almost brained one of the cunning'st fencers,
That practised with him.

JULIO
Very certain; and now you talk of fencing,
Do not you remember the Welsh gentleman,

21 *as for* ed. (for as Q)
28 *discover* watch
29 *event* result
 5 *the Dane* i.e., Contarino

[Act v, Scene iv] This scene is set in a room in Castel Nuovo.

That was travelling to Rome upon return?   15
PROSPERO
No, what of him?
JULIO
There was a strange experiment of a fencer.
PROSPERO
What was that?
JULIO
The Welshman in's play, do what the fencer could,
Hung still an arse; he could not for's life   20
Make him come on bravely: till one night at supper,
Observing what a deal of Parma cheese
His scholar devoured, goes ingeniously
The next morning, and makes a spacious button
For his foil of toasted cheese, and as sure as you live,   25
That made him come on the braveliest.
PROSPERO   .   Possible!
JULIO
Marry, it taught him an ill grace in's play,
It made him gape still, gape as he put in for't,
As I have seen some hungry usher.
PROSPERO   The toasting of it belike,
Was to make it more supple, had he chanced   30
To have hit him o'th' chaps.
JULIO   Not unlikely. Who can tell me,
If we may breathe in the devil?
PROSPERO   By no means.
JULIO
Nor drink?
PROSPERO   Neither.

---

20 *Hung still an arse* still held back
23 *goes* Q ([a] goes Lucas)
24 *button* disc fixed on the end of a fencing foil to prevent serious injury
28 *put in for't* made his thrusts (Lucas)
29 *usher* schoolmaster's assistant (usually underpaid)
31 *chaps* jaws   32 *breathe* rest to regain breath (Gunby)

---

15 *upon return* Lucas indicates that this refers 'to the curious custom practised by Elizabethan travellers, of gambling on their risks—a kind of inverted insurance. The traveller paid down a certain sum at his departure; if he failed to return, the agent kept it; if he did return, he received the amount of his deposit several times over' (Lucas, II, 359).
19–26 This joke about the Welshman's response to cheese is an old one: see Lucas, II, 360.

JULIO
That's scurvy; anger will make me very dry.
PROSPERO
You mistake sir, 'tis sorrow that is very dry.   35
SANITONELLA
Not always sir, I have known sorrow very wet.
JULIO
In rainy weather?
SANITONELLA
No, when a woman has come dropping wet
Out of a cucking-stool.
JULIO   Then 'twas wet indeed, sir.

Enter ROMELIO *very melancholy, and the* CAPUCHIN

CAPUCHIN [*aside*]
Having from Leonora's waiting-woman   40
Delivered a most strange intelligence
Of Contarino's recovery, I am come
To sound Romelio's penitence; that performed,
To end these errors by discovering
What she related to me. [*To* ROMELIO] Peace to you, sir.   45
Pray gentlemen, let the freedom of this room
Be mine a little. [*To* JULIO] Nay sir, you may stay.
                        Exeunt PRO[SPERO *and*] SAN[ITONELLA]
Will you pray with me?
ROMELIO   No, no, the world and I
Have not made up our accounts yet.
CAPUCHIN   Shall I pray for you?
ROMELIO
Whether you do or no, I care not.   50
CAPUCHIN
Oh you have a dangerous voyage to take.
ROMELIO
No matter, I will be mine own pilot:
Do not you trouble your head with the business.
CAPUCHIN
Pray tell me, do not you meditate of death?

39 *cucking-stool* stool at the end of a pole for the punishment of
    scolds by ducking in the village pond

34–5 According to the doctrine of the four humours choler was considered
    to be hot and dry; melancholy, cold and dry. The association of sorrow
    and thirst was proverbial: see Tilley, S 656.

ROMELIO
    Phew, I took out that lesson   55
    When I once lay sick of an ague: I do now
    Labour for life, for life. Sir, can you tell me,
    Whether your Toledo, or your Milan blade
    Be best tempered?
CAPUCHIN   These things, you know,
    Are out of my practice.
ROMELIO   But these are things, you know, 60
    I must practise with tomorrow.
CAPUCHIN   Were I in your case,
    I should present to myself strange shadows.
ROMELIO
    Turn you; were I in your case, I should laugh
    At mine own shadow.
    Who has hired you to make me coward?
CAPUCHIN   I would make you 65
    A good Christian.
ROMELIO   Withal, let me continue
    An honest man, which I am very certain
    A coward can never be; you take upon you
    A physician's place, rather than a divine's.
    You go about to bring my body so low,   70
    I should fight i'th' lists tomorrow like a dormouse,
    And be made away in a slumber.
CAPUCHIN   Did you murder Contarino?
ROMELIO
    That's a scurvy question now.
CAPUCHIN   Why sir?
ROMELIO
    Did you ask it as a confessor, or as a spy?
CAPUCHIN
    As one that fain would jostle the devil   75
    Out of your way.
ROMELIO   Um, you are but weakly made for't:
    He's a cunning wrestler, I can tell you, and has broke

---

55 *took out* learnt
58 *Milan* the accent falls on the first syllable
64 *own* ed. (one Q)

57–9 cf. *The White Devil*, V. vi, 231–2:
      FLAMINEO   O what blade is't?
    A toledo, or an English fox?

Many a man's neck.
CAPUCHIN   But to give him the foil,
  Goes not by strength.
ROMELIO   Let it go by what it will,
  Get me some good victuals to breakfast, I am hungry.   80
CAPUCHIN
  Here's food for you.   *Offering him a book*
ROMELIO   Phew! I am not to commence doctor:
  For then the word 'Devour that book!' were proper.
  I am to fight, to fight sir, and I'll do't,
  As I would feed, with a good stomach.
CAPUCHIN   Can you feed,
  And apprehend death?
ROMELIO   Why sir? Is not death   85
  A hungry companion? Say, is not the grave
  Said to be a great devourer? Give me some victuals.
  I knew a man that was to lose his head,
  Feed with an excellent good appetite,
  To strengthen his heart, scarce half an hour before.   90
  And if he did it, that only was to speak,
  What should I, that am to do?
CAPUCHIN   This confidence,
  If it be grounded upon truth, 'tis well.
ROMELIO
  You must understand, that resolution
  Should ever wait upon a noble death,   95
  As captains bring their soldiers out o'th' field,
  And come off last: for, I pray, what is death?
  The safest trench i'th' world to keep man free
  From fortune's gunshot; to be afraid of that,
  Would prove me weaker than a teeming woman,   100

81 *Phew!* ed. (Pew, Q); *commence doctor* take a doctor's degree
82 *word* command
84 *good stomach* good appetite
85 *apprehend* fully understand
91 *to speak* i.e., his last words
92 *to do* i.e., to fight to the death

100 *teeming woman* Lucas (II, 361) points out that this concept comes from
    Euripides, *Medea*, lines 248–51, which read, in translation:
        Men say we women lead a sheltered life
        At home, while they face death amid the spears:
        Fools! I had rather stand in the battle-line
        Thrice, than once bear a child.

That does endure a thousand times more pain
In bearing of a child.
CAPUCHIN   Oh, I tremble for you:
For I do know you have a storm within you,
More terrible than a sea-fight, and your soul
Being heretofore drowned in security,   105
You know not how to live, nor how to die:
But I have an object that shall startle you,
And make you know whither you are going.
ROMELIO
I am armed for't.

Enter LEONORA *with two coffins borne by her servants, and two*
winding-sheets stuck with flowers, presents one to her son, and the
other to JULIO

'Tis very welcome; this is a decent garment   110
Will never be out of fashion. I will kiss it.

All the flowers of the spring
Meet to perfume our burying:
These have but their growing prime
And man does flourish but his time.   115
Survey our progress from our birth:
We are set, we grow, we turn to earth.
Courts adieu, and all delights,   *Soft music*
All bewitching appetites;
Sweetest breath, and clearest eye,   120
Like perfumes go out and die;
And consequently this is done,
As shadows wait upon the sun.
Vain the ambition of kings,
Who seek by trophies and dead things,   125
To leave a living name behind,
And weave but nets to catch the wind.

Oh you have wrought a miracle, and melted
A heart of adamant! You have comprised

114 *but their growing prime* only their springtime of growth
117 *set* planted; *turn to* move towards; turn into
122 *consequently* in sequence; in succession

127 *weave but nets to catch the wind* Dent (p. 314) indicates that this was a
     well-known concept, found as a proverb (see Tilley, W 416) and in many
     of the authors most used by Webster, but Webster's 'weave' seems to
     be original.

In this dumb pageant a right excellent form 130
Of penitence.
CAPUCHIN I am glad you so receive it.
ROMELIO
This object does persuade me to forgive
The wrong she has done me, which I count the way
To be forgiven yonder: and this shroud
Shows me how rankly we do smell of earth, 135
When we are in all our glory. Will it please you *To his mother*
Enter that closet, where I shall confer
'Bout matters of most weighty consequence,
Before the duel? *Exit* LEONORA [*to the closet*]
JULIO
Now I am right in the bandoleer for th' gallows. 140
What a scurvy fashion 'tis, to hang one's coffin in a scarf!
CAPUCHIN
Why, this is well:
And now that I have made you fit for death,
And brought you even as low as is the grave,
I will raise you up again, speak comforts to you 145
Beyond your hopes, turn this intended duel
To a triumph.
ROMELIO More divinity yet?
Good sir, do one thing first: there's in my closet
A prayer-book that is covered with gilt vellum;
Fetch it, and pray you certify my mother, 150
I'll presently come to her.

[*Exit* CAPUCHIN *to the closet;* ROMELIO] *locks him in*

So now you are safe.

134 *yonder* i.e., in heaven: cf. *The Duchess of Malfi*, I. ii, 291–4
136 s.d. opposite ll. 132–3 in Q
140 *bandoleer* broad belt for cartridges worn over the shoulders and
across the breast
151 *presently* immediately; s.d. ed. (*Lockes him into a Closet.* Q)

132–4 There is a reference here to the Lord's Prayer: and Christ's comment
upon it: see St Matthew, vi, 12: 'And forgive us our debts, as we forgive
our debtors'; vi, 15: 'For if ye forgive men their trespasses, your
heavenly Father will also forgive you'.
140 Lucas comments: 'To make Julio's remarks intelligible one must im-
agine some by-play in which he takes the winding-sheet from the
coffin and puts it over his shoulder like a scarf; in this pose he wryly
compares himself to a felon bound for the gallows and wearing his
halter' (Lucas, II, 362).

JULIO
  What have you done?
ROMELIO   Why, I have locked them up
  Into a turret of the castle, safe enough
  For troubling us this four hours; and he please,
  He may open up a casement, and whistle out to th' sea,   155
  Like a bosun; not any creature can hear him.
  Wast not thou a-weary of his preaching?
JULIO
  Yes; if he had had an hour-glass by him,
  I would have wished he would have jogged it a little.
  But your mother, your mother's locked in too.   160
ROMELIO
  So much the better;
  I am rid of her howling at parting.
JULIO
  Hark, he knocks to be let out and he were mad.
ROMELIO
  Let him knock till his sandals fly in pieces.
JULIO
  Ha! What says he? Contarino living?   165
ROMELIO
  Ay, ay, he means he would have Contarino's living
  Bestowed upon his monastery; 'tis that
  He only fishes for. So, 'tis break of day;
  We shall be called to the combat presently.
JULIO
  I am sorry for one thing.
ROMELIO   What's that?   170
JULIO
  That I made not mine own ballad: I do fear
  I shall be roguishly abused in metre
  If I miscarry. Well, if the young Capuchin
  Do not talk o'th' flesh as fast now to your mother,

154 *and he* if he
156 *bosun* boatswain
159 *he* ed. (him he Q): see Textual Appendix A
163 *and he* as if he
166 *living* the parish in Contarino's gift
167–8 *'tis that/He only* 'tis only that he
173 *miscarry* meet with death

171–3 The ballads which were written about any criminal at this time were
       in very poor doggerel verse.

As he did to us o'th' spirit! If he do,   175
'Tis not the first time that the prison royal
Has been guilty of close committing.
ROMELIO   Now to th' combat.
                                              [*Exeunt*]

[Act V, Scene v]

Enter CAPUCHIN *and* LEONORA *above at a window*

LEONORA
    Contarino living?
CAPUCHIN
    Yes madam, he is living, and Ercole's second.
LEONORA
    Why has he locked us up thus?
CAPUCHIN   Some evil angel
    Makes him deaf to his own safety: we are shut
    Into a turret, the most desolate prison   5
    Of all the castle, and his obstinacy,
    Madness, or secret fate, has thus prevented
    The saving of his life.
LEONORA   Oh the saving Contarino's!
    His is worth nothing: for heaven's sake call louder.
CAPUCHIN
    To little purpose.
LEONORA   I will leap these battlements,   10
    And may I be found dead time enough
    To hinder the combat!
CAPUCHIN   Oh look upwards rather,
    Their deliverance must come thence: to see how heaven
    Can invert man's firmest purpose! His intent
    Of murdering Contarino was a mean   15
    To work his safety, and my coming hither
    To save him, is his ruin; wretches turn
    The tide of their good fortune, and being drenched
    In some presumptuous and hidden sins,

---

177 *close* (i) secret; (ii) enclosed within walls; *committing* committing
    adultery
[Act V, Scene v] Dyce, Hazlitt; Lucas continues Act V, Scene iv

---

    This scene takes place on the upper stage, representing a turret of
Castel Nuovo, above the apartment in which the previous scene was set.

6 * *

While they aspire to do themselves most right,   20
The devil that rules i'th' air, hangs in their light.
LEONORA
Oh they must not be lost thus; some good Christian
Come within our hearing! Ope the other casement
That looks into the city.
CAPUCHIN   Madam, I shall.   *Exeunt*

[Act V, Scene vi]

The lists set up. Enter the MARSHAL, CRISPIANO, *and* ARIOSTO
as judges; they sit. [*Enter* SANITONELLA, *a* HERALD *and*
ATTENDANTS]
MARSHAL
Give the appellant his summons, do the like
To the defendant.
                    Two tuckets by several trumpets.
Enter at one door, ERCOLE *and* CONTARINO, *at the other,*
ROMELIO *and* JULIO

Can any of you allege aught, why the combat
Should not proceed?
COMBATANTS   Nothing.
ARIOSTO   Have the knights weighed
And measured their weapons?
MARSHAL   They have.   5
ARIOSTO
Proceed then to the battle, and may heaven
Determine the right.
HERALD
Soit la bataille, et victoire à ceux qui ont droit.
ROMELIO
Stay, I do not well know whither I am going:
'Twere needful therefore, though at the last gasp,   10

[**Act V, Scene vi**] Dyce, Hazlitt ([ACTUS QUINTUS, SCENA QUINTA.]
    Lucas)
2 s.d. *tuckets* trumpet signals
8 *Soit . . . droit.* Let the battle commence, and victory to those who
    are in the right.

20–1 Cf. *The Duchess of Malfi*, II. i, 97–8: Lucas (II, 147) pointed out that
    the Bishops' Bible version of Ephesians, ii, 2 said that the devil 'ruleth in
    the ayre' and consequently the phrase became proverbial.
[Act V, Scene vi This scene takes place outside Castel Nuovo and is
presented on the outer stage.

To have some churchman's prayer. Run, I pray thee,
To Castle Nuovo; this key will release
A Capuchin and my mother, whom I shut
Into a turret, – bid them make haste, and pray, –
I may be dead ere he comes.   [*Exit an* ATTENDANT]   15
Now, *Victoire à ceux qui ont droit.*

ALL THE CHAMP
Victoire à ceux qui ont droit.

The combat continued to a good length, when enters LEONORA,
and the CAPUCHIN

LEONORA
Hold, hold, for heaven's sake hold.

ARIOSTO
What are these that interrupt the combat?
Away to prison with them.
CAPUCHIN   We have been prisoners too long.   20
Oh sir, what mean you? Contarino's living.

ERCOLE
Living!
CAPUCHIN Behold him living.   [CONTARINO *reveals himself*]

ERCOLE
You were but now my second, now I make you
Myself for ever.   [*They lean across* LEONORA *to embrace*]
LEONORA   Oh here's one between,
Claims to be nearer.
CONTARINO   And to you, dear lady,   25
I have entirely vowed my life.
ROMELIO   If I do not
Dream, I am happy too.
ARIOSTO   How insolently
Has this high Court of Honour been abused!

Enter ANGIOLELLA *veiled, and* JOLENTA, *her face coloured like a
Moor, the* TWO SURGEONS, *one of them like a Jew*

17 s.p. ALL THE CHAMP 'All the spectators in the *champ* or field of
    battle' (Hazlitt); Lucas (II, 362) thinks that the other combatants
    are intended
24 s.d. this ed. ([*They embrace.*] Lucas)

25–6 Lucas (II, 362–3) comments on this denouement as strange both in
    the pairing off of Contarino and Leonora and in the doubts about it
    raised by the obscurity of the printed text.

ARIOSTO
How now, who are these?

SECOND SURGEON
A couple of strange fowl, and I the falconer,   30
That have sprung them. This is a white nun,
Of the Order of St Clare; and this is a black one,
You'll take my word for't.   *Discovers* JOLENTA

ARIOSTO   She's a black one indeed.

JOLENTA
                    Like or dislike me, choose you whether:
                    The down upon the raven's feather,   35
                    Is as gentle and as sleek,
                    As the mole on Venus' cheek.
                    Hence vain show! I only care,
                    To preserve my soul most fair,
                    Never mind the outward skin,   40
                    But the jewel that's within:
                    And though I want the crimson blood,
                    Angels boast my sisterhood.
                    Which of us now judge you whiter:
                    Her whose credit proves the lighter,   45
                    Or this black and ebon hue
                    That, unstained, keeps fresh and true?
                    For I proclaim't without control,
                    There's no true beauty, but i'th' soul.

ERCOLE
Oh 'tis the fair Jolenta! To what purpose   50
Are you thus eclipsed?

JOLENTA   Sir, I was running away
From the rumour of the combat: I fled likewise,
From the untrue report my brother spread
To his politic ends, that I was got with child.

LEONORA
Cease here all further scrutiny; this paper   55
Shall give unto the court each circumstance
Of all these passages.

31 *sprung* started from their cover
32 *Order of St Clare*: see III. iii, 35n
42 *crimson blood* red cheeks: cf. *The White Devil*, V. vi, 224–8
45 *credit . . . lighter* (i) reputation; (ii) value when weighed in the
    balance
48 *control* reservation (Gunby)
51 *eclipsed* obscured, i.e., with a dark stain on the skin
54 *politic* scheming   57 *passages* events

ARIOSTO
No more: attend the sentence of the court.
Rareness and difficulty give estimation
To all things are i'th' world: you have met both   60
In these several passages; now it does remain,
That these so comical events be blasted
With no severity of sentence. You, Romelio,
Shall first deliver to that gentleman,
Who stood your second, all those obligations   65
Wherein he stands engaged to you, receiving
Only the principal.
ROMELIO   I shall, my lord.
JULIO   I thank you:
I have an humour now to go to sea
Against the pirates; and my only ambition
Is to have my ship furnished with a rare consort   70
Of music; and when I am pleased to be mad,
They shall play me *Orlando*.
SANITONELLA
You must lay wait for the fiddlers,
They'll fly away from the press like watermen.
ARIOSTO
Next, you shall marry that nun.
ROMELIO   Most willingly.   75
ANGIOLELLA
Oh sir, you have been unkind;
But I do only wish, that this my shame
May warn all honest virgins, not to seek
The way to heaven, that is so wondrous steep,
Thorough those vows they are too frail to keep.   80

58 *attend* listen to
62 *blasted* cursed
65 *obligations* agreements, enforceable by law, whereby a person is
    bound to pay a certain sum of money to another
70 *consort* concert, a small collection of instruments
72 *Orlando   Orlando Furioso* (Orlando in Madness): Ariosto's epic
    poem had been popularized by translation into English by Sir
    John Harington, in 1591, and dramatization by Robert Greene
80 *Thorough* Dyce, Lucas (Through Q, Hazlitt)

59–60: From Montaigne, II, xv: '*Rarenes and difficulties giveth esteeme unto
    things*' (Lucas and Dent).
74–5 'Watermen with a knowledge of boat handling sought ways to escape
    being impressed into the navy' (Shirley).

ARIOSTO

    Contarino, and Romelio, and yourself,
Shall for seven years maintain against the Turk
Six galleys. Leonora, Jolenta,
And Angiolella there, the beauteous nun,
For their vows' breach unto the monastery,   85
Shall build a monastery. Lastly, the two surgeons,
For concealing Contarino's recovery,
Shall exercise their art at their own charge
For a twelvemonth in the galleys: so we leave you,
Wishing your future life may make good use   90
Of these events, since that these passages,
Which threatened ruin, built on rotten ground,
Are with success beyond our wishes crowned.

                                          Exeunt omnes

FINIS

81 *Romelio* Qb (Romelto Qa); *yourself* i.e., Ercole
88 *charge* expense

Textual Appendices

Textual Appendix A

COLLATIONS AND GENERAL NOTES ON THE TEXT

The Actors' Names
   12 CONTILUPO ed. (*Cantilupoe* Q)

To the Judicious Reader
   8 *citharæ* ed. (Citheræ Q)

[Act I, Scene i]
   14 *trading?* ed. (Trading, Q)
   17 *Baptista's* ed. (*Baptisto's* Q)
   54 *others'* ed. (other Q): the emendation is substantiated by
      reference to Webster's source for the passage
  139 *withal* Qb (wityal Qa)

[Act I, Scene ii]
  112 *hearty?* ed. (heartie. Q; hearty, – Dyce; hearty – Hazlitt;
      heartie . . . Lucas)
  162 *and mantoons* ed. (and Man-oons Qa; & Man-toons Qb)
  161 *corn-cutting* ed. (Cornecutting Qa; Corne-cutting Qb)
185–6 *I do but jest; thou knowest, wit and a woman,*
     Are two very frail things; and so I leave you.
     Q's punctuation –
     I do but jest, thou knowest, wit and a woman
     Are two very frail things, and so I leave you.
     – may be alternatively modernized:
     I do but jest, thou knowest; wit and a woman
     Are two very frail things: and so I leave you.

[Act II, Scene i]
  239 *'T has* Dyce, Hazlitt ('Tas Q; 'Tis Lucas)

[Act II, Scene iv]
  17 *Sicil* Dyce (Cicil Q; [S]icil Lucas; Sicily Hazlitt)

[Act III, Scene ii]
  32 *ta'en?* ed. (tane. Q)
  78 *death!* ed. (death: Q)

[Act IV, Scene i]
  23 *enough* ed. (enow Q)

[Act IV, Scene ii]

  43 s.d. *Enter* CRISPIANO Q, Hazlitt, Lucas (*Enter, at one bar*
       CRISPIANO Dyce); *lawyer* ... LEONORA Q, Hazlitt, Lucas
       (*lawyer; at another bar*, ROMELIO, ARIOSTO, LEONORA Dyce)

  44 *suit: is* ed. (Suite, is Q; suit. – Is Dyce; suit. Is Hazlitt;
       Suite – is Lucas)

 118 *Fieschi* ed. (*Fliski* Q); *Doria* ed. (*Dori* Q)

 275 *lose* ed. (loose Q)

 384 *me; which I took, he* ed. (mee, which I tooke; he Q; me,
       – which I took; he Dyce; me; which, I took he Hazlitt;
       mee; which I tooke he Lucas)

 410 *remembered* ed. (remembred Q)

 460 *bleared* Lucas (bleated Q, Dyce, Hazlitt, Shirley)

 566 *duel?* ed. (Duell. Q)

[Act V, Scene iv]

  18 s.p. PROSPERO ed. (*Pras.* Q)

  78 *Many* ed. (many Q)

 159 *he* Lucas (him he Q, Dyce, Hazlitt); Lucas comments, '*him*
       may be a relic of an alternative version – *I would have wisht
       him to have jogg'd it a little*'.

Textual Appendix B

VARIANT READINGS WHICH AFFECT THE VERSE STRUCTURE OF THE PLAY

NOTE: for ease of reference, the spelling and punctuation of this edition are used throughout this appendix

I. i, 1–3   Q prints as four lines, dividing at ... *wealth;| ... merchant| ... substance.| ... Spain|*; Dyce and Lucas print as four lines, dividing ... *think| ... Italy| ... substance.| ... Spain|*; Hazlitt prints as five lines, dividing ... *wealth;| ... think| ... merchant| ... substance.| ... Spain|*.

16–18   Q, Dyce, Hazlitt and Lucas print as six lines.

23   Q, Dyce, Hazlitt and Lucas print as two lines.

26–7   Q and Hazlitt print as two lines, dividing ... *Contarino.| ... sister.|*; Dyce and Lucas print as three lines, dividing ... *Contarino.| ... know| ... sister.|*.

30   Q, Dyce, Hazlitt and Lucas print as two lines.

40–1   Q and Hazlitt print as three lines, dividing ... *value.| ... it.| ... were|*; Dyce and Lucas print as four lines, dividing ... *value.| ... her| ... it.| ... were|*.

46   Q, Dyce, Hazlitt and Lucas print as two lines.

49–50   Q prints as three lines, dividing ... *it?| ... travel?| ... lose|*; Dyce and Hazlitt print as four lines, dividing ... *it?| ... travel?| No.| ... lose|*; Lucas prints as three lines, dividing ... *it?| ... you| ... lose|*.

51a   A single line in Q, Dyce, Hazlitt and Lucas.

51b–54a   Q prints as prose; Dyce and Lucas print as four lines of verse, dividing ... *heard| ... Alps,| ... rate| ... vices.|*; Hazlitt prints as three lines of verse, dividing ... *Alps,| ... rate| ... vices.|*.

54, 66   Q, Dyce, Hazlitt and Lucas print as two lines.

69–71   Q and Hazlitt print as four lines, dividing ... *aim it.| ... sir?| ... wedding.| ... lord?|*; Dyce and Lucas print as six lines, dividing ... *bonds,| ... aim it.| ... sir?| ... it| ... wedding.| ... lord?|*.

81, 103   Q, Dyce, Hazlitt and Lucas print as two lines.

115   Q, Hazlitt and Lucas print as two lines; Dyce prints as one line.

120–3　Q and Hazlitt print as five lines, dividing . . . *service.|
. . . favours.| . . . it.| . . . in,| . . . breath.|*; Dyce prints
as seven lines, dividing . . . *service.| . . . you| . . .
favours.| . . . you| . . . it.| . . . got| . . . breath.|*; Lucas
prints as seven lines, dividing . . . *service.| . . . you|
. . . favours.| . . . fame| . . . it.| . . . got| . . . breath.|*.

134–7　Q prints as six lines, dividing . . . *already.| . . . your|
. . . me.| summer,| . . . leaf.| . . . time;|*; Dyce and
Lucas print as seven lines, dividing . . . *already.| . . .
bounty.| . . . me.| . . . sir,| . . . me,| . . . leaf.| . . .
time;|*; Hazlitt prints as six lines, dividing . . .
*already.| . . . bestow| . . . me.| . . . summer,| . . . leaf.|
. . . time;|*.

141　Q, Dyce, Hazlitt and Lucas print as two lines.

155　Q, Dyce, Hazlitt and Lucas print as three lines.

163, 166　Q, Dyce, Hazlitt and Lucas print as two lines.

171　Q, Dyce, Hazlitt and Lucas print as three lines.

185–6　Q divides . . . *pearched!| I* . . .; Dyce and Lucas
divide . . . *hope|You* . . .; Hazlitt divides . . . *pearched
on!|I* . . .

192　Q prints as one line; Dyce prints 192a as one line;
192b–193 as prose; Hazlitt prints 192–4 as prose;
Lucas prints as two lines.

I. ii, 2–6　Q and Hazlitt print as seven lines, dividing . . .
*clothes.| . . . coffin.| . . . Look you,| . . . greets you.| . . .
me?| . . . now.| . . . I pray?|*; Dyce and Lucas print
as ten lines, dividing . . . *clothes.| . . . maker,| . . .
coffin.| Tomb-maker?| . . . greets you.| . . . mean?| . . .
me?| . . . come,| . . . now.| . . . I pray?|*.

9–11　Q and Hazlitt print as three lines, dividing . . .
husband.| . . . my| . . . myself.|; Dyce and Lucas
print as four lines, dividing . . . *husband.| . . . season:|
. . . stretched| . . . myself.|*.

13–14　Q, Dyce, Hazlitt and Lucas print as four lines.

16　Q, Dyce, Hazlitt and Lucas print as two lines.

32–3　Q and Hazlitt print as three lines, dividing . . .
fortune.| . . . you?| . . . brother.|; Dyce and Lucas
print as four lines, dividing . . . *fortune.| . . . hither:|
. . . you?| . . . brother.|*.

41, 45　Q, Dyce, Hazlitt and Lucas print as two lines.

47　Q and Lucas print as two lines, dividing . . . *breeding.|
. . . me|*; Dyce and Hazlitt print as three lines.

55, 61, 86　Q, Dyce, Hazlitt and Lucas print as two lines.

88–94　Q and Hazlitt print as eight lines, dividing . . .

husband.| . . . for you,| . . . soul;| . . . please.| . . . nobly.| . . . do?| . . . Contarino,| . . . dwell|; Dyce and Lucas print as ten lines, dividing *. . . husband.| . . . do| . . . leave you| . . . whither| . . . please.| . . . yourself| . . . nobly.| . . . do?| . . . Contarino,| . . . dwell.*

95–9 Q prints as seven lines, dividing *. . . thee.| . . . intended| . . . purpose.| . . . ever.| . . . hand.| . . . sir.| . . . then:|*; Dyce, Hazlitt and Lucas print as seven lines, but divide the second at *. . . never|Intended . . .*

102–14 Q and Hazlitt print as sixteen lines, dividing *. . . viol!| . . . art.| . . . cunning,| . . . away,| . . . soul.| . . . regarded,| . . . appearance| . . . sunshine.| . . . yours.| . . . in|dumb . . .* [prose] *. . . her.| . . . fashionable.| . . . hearty?| . . . unwilling.| . . . observe the| . . . contracts,|*; Dyce prints as eighteen lines, dividing *. . . teach| . . . art.| . . . cunning,| . . . away,| . . . soul.| . . . lord,| . . . maidenheads| . . . appearance| . . . sunshine.| . . . yours.| . . . deal you| . . . of her.| . . . fashionable.| . . . hearty?| . . . unwilling.| . . . else?| . . . the like| . . . contracts,|*; Lucas prints as nineteen lines, dividing *. . . teach| . . . art.| . . . cunning,| . . . away,| . . . soul.| . . . lord,| . . . maidenheads| . . . crying,| . . . sunshine.| . . . yours.| . . . show;| . . . of her.| . . . contracted| . . . fashionable.| . . . suppose| . . . hearty?| . . . unwilling.| . . . observe| . . . contracts;|.*

116, 120, 137, 149 Q, Dyce, Hazlitt and Lucas print as two lines.

151–2 Q prints as three lines, dividing *. . . husband.| Husband?| . . . arrived at.|*; Dyce and Lucas print as four lines, dividing *. . . husband.|Husband?| . . . is| . . . at.|*; Hazlitt prints as four lines, dividing *. . . husband.|Husband?| . . . that| . . . at.|.*

158, 171 Q, Dyce, Hazlitt and Lucas print as two lines.

175–6 Q, Dyce, Hazlitt and Lucas divide *. . . travelled| Indeed . . .*

181 Q, Dyce, Hazlitt and Lucas print as two lines.

197–8 Q and Hazlitt print as three lines, dividing *. . . bad enough.| . . . of 't.| . . . mistress?|*; Dyce and Lucas print as four lines, dividing *. . . bad enough.| . . . hope| . . . of 't.| . . . mistress?|.*

206, 208 Q, Dyce, Hazlitt and Lucas print as two lines.

210–11 Q, Dyce, Hazlitt and Lucas print as verse, dividing *. . . share|In . . .*

212 Q, Dyce, Hazlitt and Lucas print as three lines.

217–18 Q, Dyce, Hazlitt and Lucas print as three lines,
dividing ... *so!*| ... *means*| ... *me?*|.

221, 227 Q, Dyce, Hazlitt and Lucas print as two lines.

231–2 Q prints as two lines, dividing ... *breathed*| ...
opinion,|; Dyce, Hazlitt and Lucas print as three
lines, dividing ... *on't.*| ... *together!*| ... *opinion,*|.

244, 248 Q, Dyce, Hazlitt and Lucas print as two lines.

255–61 Q and Hazlitt print as ten lines, dividing ... *this.*|
... *none.*| ... *honour?*| ... *Ercole?*| ... *guiltless.*| ...
yourself.| ... *mother?*| ... *women.*| ... *married.*| ...
union|; Dyce prints as eleven lines, dividing ...
quarrel| ... *this.*| ... *none.*| ... *honour?*| ... *Ercole?*|
... *guiltless.*| ... *yourself.*| ... *mother?*| ... *women.*|
... *married.*| ... *union*|; Lucas prints as ten lines,
dividing ... *quarrel*| ... *this.*| ... *none.*| *None,*| ...
honour?| ... *Ercole?*| ... *brother?*| ... *mother?*| ...
we'll| ... *union*|.

II. i, 7–8 Q, Hazlitt and Lucas print as verse; Dyce prints as
prose.

16–17 Q, Dyce, Hazlitt and Lucas print as four lines.

50–3 Q and Hazlitt print as four lines, dividing *Possible?*|
... *law.*| ... *sir?*| ... *other.*|; Dyce and Lucas print
as six lines, dividing *Possible?*| ... *like,*| ... *law.*|
... *sir?*| ... *familiar*| ... *other.*|.

62, 64, 67, 74 Q, Dyce, Hazlitt and Lucas print as two lines.

75–7 Q, Dyce, Hazlitt and Lucas print as four lines,
dividing ... *chimneys,*| ... *tunnels*| ... *beget*| ...
fundaments.|.

85–6 Q and Dyce print as three lines, dividing ... *he?*| ...
with,| ... *merchant.*|; Dyce prints as three lines,
dividing ... *he?*| ... *Romelio*| ... *merchant.*|; Lucas
prints as three lines, dividing ... *he?*| ... *gentleman*|
... *merchant.*|.

92, 94, 99 Q, Dyce, Hazlitt and Lucas print as two lines.

104–5 Q, Dyce and Hazlitt print as prose; Lucas prints as
verse, dividing ... *profession*| *I* ...

107–8 Q and Lucas print as two lines of verse, dividing ...
hope,| ... *sir.*|; Dyce prints as three lines of verse,
dividing ... *hope,*| ... *heir.*| ... *sir.*|; Hazlitt
prints as prose.

109–12 Q and Hazlitt print as verse, dividing ... *question.*|
... *action,*| ... *merry*;| ... *tidings.*|; Dyce and Lucas
print as prose.

144-5   Q, Hazlitt and Lucas print as verse, dividing . . . *sir,/*
         'Twill . . .; Dyce prints as prose.

147   Q, Dyce, Hazlitt and Lucas print as two lines.

153-9   Q and Hazlitt print as verse, dividing . . . *great/* . . .
         officers./ . . . *spent/* . . . *allowance?/* . . . *allowance?/* . . .
         begat me?/ . . . *end?/*; Dyce and Lucas print as prose.

164-5   Q and Hazlitt print as verse, dividing . . . *stockings,/*
         With . . .; Dyce and Lucas print as prose.

171-2   Q and Hazlitt print as verse, dividing . . . *velvet,/*
         With . . .; Dyce and Lucas print as prose.

173-4   Q and Hazlitt print as verse, dividing . . . *upon/Cow*
         . . .; Dyce and Lucas print as prose.

183-5   [*and apricocks* . . . *sieve, and*]: Q prints as verse,
         dividing . . . *spring,/* . . . *with./* . . . *young/*; Dyce,
         Hazlitt and Lucas print as prose.

199-200 Q prints as verse, dividing . . . *barber,/He* . . .;
         Dyce, Hazlitt and Lucas print as prose.

209-11   Q prints as prose; Dyce, Hazlitt and Lucas print as
         four lines of verse, dividing . . . *long:/* . . . *galleys/* . . .
         about./ . . . *Ercole,/.*

213   Q and Lucas print as two lines, dividing . . . *sir?/*
         Only . . .; Dyce and Hazlitt print as three lines.

218   Q, Dyce, Hazlitt and Lucas print as two lines.

225   Q, Hazlitt and Lucas print as three lines; Dyce
         prints as three lines, dividing 224-5 . . . *hearty/On* . . .

237-8   Q prints as three lines, dividing . . . *all./* . . . *you./* . . .
         voyage./; Dyce, Hazlitt and Lucas print as three lines
         dividing . . . *all./* . . . *prove/* . . . *voyage./.*

239   Q and Hazlitt print as two lines, dividing . . . *mighty./*
         . . . *heaven/*; Dyce and Lucas print as two lines,
         dividing . . . *mighty./* . . . *seal/.*

247   Q, Dyce, Hazlitt and Lucas print as two lines.

248   Q, Dyce, Hazlitt and Lucas print as three lines.

250-1   Q and Hazlitt print as four lines, dividing . . .
         marriage./ . . . *me./ Why?/* . . . *truth,/*; Dyce and
         Lucas print as five lines, dividing . . . *marriage./* . . .
         truth,/ . . . *me/Why?/* . . . *truth,/.*

261   Q and Lucas print as two lines, dividing . . . *me./I* . . .;
         Dyce and Hazlitt print as three lines.

269-70   Q and Hazlitt print as three lines, dividing . . .
         enemy./ . . . *quarrel./* . . . *quarrel?/*; Dyce and Lucas
         print as four lines, dividing . . . *enemy./* . . . *me-*
         thinks,/ . . . *quarrel./* . . . *quarrel?/.*

272-3   Q prints as three lines, dividing . . . *scholar./* . . .

terrible,| . . . it|; Dyce and Lucas print as three lines, dividing . . . *scholar.| . . . ornament| . . . it|*; Hazlitt prints as three lines, dividing . . . *scholar.| . . . terrible,| . . . attended on|*.

280–2	Q, Dyce, Hazlitt and Lucas print as six lines.

285, 289, 293, 295, 297 Q, Dyce, Hazlitt and Lucas print as two lines.

299–301	Q and Hazlitt print as four lines, dividing . . . *matter?| . . . greatest| . . . sea,| . . . leave me.|*; Dyce and Lucas print as four lines, dividing . . . *matter?| . . . poured out| . . . world| . . . leave me.|*.

302–4	Q and Hazlitt print as four lines, dividing . . . *Ercole?| . . . Contarino.|Contarino?| . . . with Ercole,|*; Dyce prints as five lines, dividing . . . *Ercole?| . . . hence,| . . . Contarino.|Contarino?| . . . entreated|*; Lucas prints as five lines, dividing . . . *Ercole?| . . . hence,| . . . Contarino.|Contarino?| . . . with Ercole,|*.

307–8	Q, Hazlitt and Lucas print as four lines, dividing . . . *alone:| . . . fight.| To fight?| . . . gentlemen,|*; Dyce prints as four lines, dividing . . . *gone| To fight.| To fight?| . . . gentlemen,|*.

II. ii, 8	Q, Dyce, Hazlitt and Lucas print as two lines.

12–13	Q, Hazlitt and Lucas print as three lines, dividing . . . *alike.| . . . ready?| . . . yourself,|*; Dyce prints as two lines, dividing . . . *ready?| . . . yourself,|*.

15, 30, 35 Q, Dyce, Hazlitt and Lucas print as two lines.

43	Q, Hazlitt and Lucas print as two lines, dividing . . . *throats|Brave* . . .; Dyce prints as one line.

II. iii, 2–5	Q prints as four lines, dividing . . . *patience.| . . . not.| . . . am| . . . you,|*; Dyce and Lucas print as six lines, dividing . . . *patience.| . . . losses| . . . not.| . . . true| . . . wished,| . . . you,|*; Hazlitt prints as four lines, dividing . . . *patience.| . . . not.| . . . wished,| . . . you,|*.

7–8	Q, Dyce, Hazlitt and Lucas print as four lines.

12–14	Q and Hazlitt print as four lines, dividing . . . *else.| . . . Julio.| . . . patience?| . . . crosses.|*; Dyce and Lucas print as four lines, dividing . . . *remember| . . . leech| . . . patience?| . . . crosses.|*.

15–16	Q, Dyce, Hazlitt and Lucas print as four lines.

23–4	Q and Lucas print as three lines, dividing . . . *merry.| . . . angry.| . . . you|*; Dyce and Hazlitt print as four lines, dividing . . . *merry.| . . . patience,| angry.| . . . you|*.

34–6   Q prints as three lines, dividing ... *divine.| ...*
        many|times [prose] ... *pray,|*; Dyce and Lucas
        print as four lines, dividing ... *divine.| ... heard|*
        ... *times| ... pray,|*; Hazlitt prints as three lines,
        dividing ... *divine.| ... much,| ... pray,|*.

48   Q, Dyce, Hazlitt and Lucas print as two lines.

53–4   Q prints as three lines, dividing ... *third,| ... sir.|*
        ... *names|*; Dyce and Hazlitt print as four lines,
        dividing ... *third| ... Leviathan?| ... sir.| ...*
        names|; Lucas prints as three lines, dividing ...
        Great| ... sir.| ... names|.

55–7   Q, Dyce and Hazlitt print as four lines, dividing ...
        think| ... mean,| ... stocks.| ... superstitious;|;
        Lucas prints as four lines, dividing ... *cursed| ...*
        were| ... stocks.| ... superstitious;|.

60–2   Q prints as four lines, dividing ... *of them,| ...*
        for't.| ... city.| ... more,|; Dyce and Hazlitt print
        as four lines, dividing ... *made them| ... handsel|*
        ... *city.| ... more,|*; Lucas prints as four lines,
        dividing ... *that| ... handsel| ... city.| ... more,|*.

73–5   Q and Hazlitt print as four lines, dividing ...
        goods.| ... thus?| ... understand| ... say.|; Dyce
        and Lucas print as four lines, dividing ... *goods.|*
        ... *ring| ... court,| ... say.|*.

85–7   Q and Hazlitt print as four lines, dividing ... *sir?|*
        ... *Contarino,| ... combat.| ... ever!|*; Dyce prints
        as five lines, dividing ... *sir?| ... Ercole,| ...*
        slain| ... combat.| ... ever!|; Lucas prints as five
        lines, dividing ... *sir?| ... Ercole,| ... them| ...*
        combat.| ... ever!|.

93, 130, 134, 139 Q, Dyce, Hazlitt and Lucas print as two
        lines.

142   Q and Lucas print as two lines, dividing ... *living.|*
        Living?; Dyce and Hazlitt print as three lines.

145, 152, 153 Q, Dyce, Hazlitt and Lucas print as two lines.

158–9   Q and Hazlitt print as three lines, dividing ... *so?|*
        ... *live,| ... law.|*; Dyce and Lucas print as three
        lines, dividing ... *so?| ... mean,| ... law.|*.

160   Q, Dyce, Hazlitt and Lucas print as two lines.

II. iv, 1–4 Q prints as prose; Dyce, Hazlitt and Lucas print as
        four lines, dividing ... *sir,| ... reason:| ... surgeons|*
        ... *you.|*.

17–18   Q and Hazlitt print as three lines, dividing ...
        Malta.| ... death?| ... life|; Dyce and Lucas print

as four lines, dividing ... *Malta.|* ... *at|* ...
death?| ... *life|.*

23, 25   Q, Dyce, Hazlitt and Lucas print as two lines.

40–2   Q and Hazlitt print as four lines, dividing ...
child.| ... *work|* ... *devil.|* ... *him,|*; Dyce and
Lucas print as five lines, dividing ... *child.|* ...
crimes| ... *repentance,|* ... *devil.|* ... *him,|.*

III. i, 1–3   Q prints as three lines, dividing ... *promise,|* ...
clouded.| ... *Spain|*; Dyce and Lucas print as four
lines, dividing ... *claim|* ... *cause|* ... *clouded.|* ...
Spain|; Hazlitt prints as three lines, dividing ...
claim| ... *clouded.|* ... *Spain|.*

25, 28   Q, Dyce, Hazlitt and Lucas print as two lines.

III. ii, 18, 22, 29   Q, Dyce, Hazlitt and Lucas print as two lines.

37–8   Q prints as three lines, dividing ... *you.|* ... *sir?|* ...
nothing.|; Dyce, Hazlitt and Lucas print as three
lines, dividing ... *you.|* ... *will,|* ... *nothing.|.*

41, 49, 61, 62, 66, 67   Q, Dyce, Hazlitt and Lucas print as
two lines.

89–90   Q divides ... *pigs!|A most* ...; Dyce, Hazlitt and
Lucas divide ... *execution| Barmotho* ...

107–8   Q prints as three lines, dividing ... *thus.|* ...
escape.| ... *mountebank,|*; Dyce, Hazlitt and Lucas
print as three lines, dividing ... *done:|* ... *escape.|*
... *mountebank,|.*

117–18   Q, Dyce and Hazlitt print as three lines, dividing ...
indeed.| ... *hither.|* ... *letter.|*; Lucas prints as four
lines, dividing ... *indeed.|* ... *why|* ... *hither.|* ...
letter.|

120–1   Q, Dyce, Hazlitt and Lucas print as four lines,
dividing ... *me.|* ... *lived|* ... *hours.|* ... *then,|.*

135–7   Q prints as two lines of prose; Dyce, Hazlitt and
Lucas print as three lines, dividing ... *surprised!|* ...
perpetually| ... *beggars.|*

145–6   Q and Lucas print as two lines, dividing ... *groan?|*
Is ...; Dyce and Hazlitt print as three lines.

150–2   Q and Hazlitt print as three lines, dividing ...
putrefaction.| ... *lively.|* ... *in't,|*; Dyce and Lucas
print as five lines, dividing ... *delivers|* ... *putre-*
faction.| ... *fetches|* ... *lively|* ... *in't,|.*

III. iii, 5, 7, 9   Q, Dyce, Hazlitt and Lucas print as two lines.

21–2   Q and Hazlitt print as three lines, dividing ...
house.| ... *foundation.|* ... *me.|*; Dyce and Lucas

print as four lines, dividing ... *house.| ... heed,| ... foundation.| ... me.|.*

29–30   Q and Hazlitt print as two lines, dividing ... *too.| ... virgin!|*; Dyce and Lucas print as three lines, dividing ... *too.| ... this?| ... virgin!|.*

41–2   Q, Hazlitt and Lucas print as three lines, dividing ... *child.| ... midwife!| ... pleasant.|*; Dyce prints as four lines, dividing ... *child.| ... work| ... midwife!| ... pleasant.|.*

51–5   Q and Hazlitt print as seven lines, dividing ... *matrimony.| ... you,| ... bastard.| ... time| ... like.| ... of it.| ... capable?|*; Dyce and Lucas print as nine lines, dividing ... *matrimony.| ... you,| ... bastard.| Right:| ... labour,| ... like| ... this,| ... of it.| ... capable?|.*

63, 66, 79, 81   Q, Dyce, Hazlitt and Lucas print as two lines.

85–6   Q divides ... *own| Sorrow* ...; Dyce, Hazlitt and Lucas divide ... *consumption| Of* ...

86b–89   Q prints as prose; Dyce and Hazlitt print as four lines, dividing ... *do:| ... me| ... unnatura^l| ... take.|*; Lucas prints as four lines, dividing ... *do:| ... me| ... falsehood:| ... tale.|.*

94, 105, 107   Q, Dyce, Hazlitt and Lucas print as two lines.

109–10   Q prints as prose; Dyce, Hazlitt and Lucas print as two lines, dividing ... *him,| Lying* ...; 110b is a separate line in Q, Dyce, Hazlitt and Lucas.

121–2   Q, Hazlitt and Lucas divide ... *upon't| He* ...; Dyce divides ... *undergone| The* ...

134–6   Q, Dyce and Hazlitt print as two lines, dividing ... *loved| ... money:|*; Lucas prints as three lines, dividing ... *lust,| ... kind,| ... money:|.*

150   Q, Dyce, Hazlitt and Lucas print as two lines.

151–3   Q and Hazlitt print as four lines, dividing ... *us| ... health,| ... him.| ... world|*; Dyce prints as three lines, dividing ... *us| health,| ... world|*; Lucas prints as three lines, dividing ... *strengthen| ... never| ... world|.*

161–2   Q, Dyce, Hazlitt and Lucas print as four lines.

170–2   Q prints 170a as a separate line; 170b–171a as prose and divides two further lines ... *noon.| ... up,|*; Dyce and Lucas print as six lines, dividing ... *swoundings.| ... oatmeal,| ... colour.| ... bed| ... noon.| ... up,|*; Hazlitt prints as five lines, dividing ... *swoundings.| ... away| ... colour.| ... noon.| ... up,|.*

174   Q, Dyce, Hazlitt and Lucas print as two lines.

181–3   Q prints as four lines, dividing ... *sorrow!| ...
        enough,| ... coat?| ... passions|*; Dyce, Hazlitt and
        Lucas print as three lines, dividing ... *now| ...
        wear| ... passions|.*

190–2   Q prints as two lines, dividing ... *law-case!| ...
        fiend|*; Dyce and Lucas print as three lines, dividing
        ... *up| ... care| ... fiend|*; Hazlitt prints as three
        lines, dividing ... *law-case!| ... be| ... fiend|.*

204–5   Q, Dyce and Hazlitt print as three lines, dividing ...
        child.| ... misfortunes| ... mischiefs|; Lucas prints
        as three lines, dividing ... *child.| ... now| ...
        mischiefs|.*

208–9   Q, Dyce and Hazlitt print as three lines, dividing ...
        Contarino?| ... skip| ... question!|; Lucas prints as
        three lines, dividing ... *Contarino?| ... you| ...
        question!|.*

213–14 Q prints 213a as a separate line; 213b–214a as prose,
        aligning *Ha?* with 214a; Dyce prints as four lines,
        dividing ... *him.| ... elder| ... lips.| Ha?|*; Hazlitt
        prints as four lines, 213a as a separate line; 213b–
        214a as two lines of prose; *Ha?* as a separate line;
        Lucas prints as three lines, dividing ... *him.| ...
        elder| ... Ha?|.*

224–7   Q prints as five lines, dividing ... *couple| ... sick.|
        ... grieved,| ... mother.| ... indeed,|*; Dyce and
        Hazlitt print as six lines, dividing ... *without| ...
        murmur.| ... sick.| ... grieved,| ... mother.| ...
        indeed,|*; Lucas prints as five lines, dividing ...
        *without| ... sick.| ... troubled| ... mother| ...
        indeed,|.*

228–31 Q, Dyce and Hazlitt print as five lines, dividing ...
        *son.| ... sister;| ... business.| ... Contarino?| ...
        heir.|*; Lucas prints as six lines, dividing ... *son.| ...
        sister;| ... business.| ... mourn| ... fit:| ... heir.|.*

243–4   Q, Dyce and Hazlitt divide ... *matron| To ...*;
        Lucas divides ... *affect| I'th' ...*

275–6   Q and Hazlitt print as three lines, dividing ...
        stubborn-hearted.| ... man,| ... me.|; Dyce and
        Lucas print as two lines, dividing ... *sink| ... me.|.*

283   Q, Dyce, Hazlitt and Lucas print as two lines.

287–90 Q prints as five lines, dividing ... *life.| ... lost.| ...
        been| ... saved,| ... live*; Dyce prints as seven lines,
        dividing ... *life.| ... me| ... lost.| ... been| ...*

saved,| . . . o'er.| . . . live|; Hazlitt prints as five lines, dividing . . . *life.| . . . lost.| . . . son-in-law:| . . . o'er.| . . . live|*; Lucas prints as six lines, dividing . . . *life.| . . . me| . . . lost.| . . . been| . . . saved,| . . . live|*.

290   Qa prints as two lines; Qb prints as one line.

295   Q, Dyce, Hazlitt and Lucas print as two lines.

297–8   Q, Dyce and Hazlitt print as two lines, dividing . . . *safety.| . . . comfort?|*; Dyce prints as three lines, dividing . . . *safety.| Where,| . . . comfort?|*.

300–1   Q prints 300–301a as prose; 301b as a separate line; Dyce and Hazlitt print as three lines, dividing . . . *man,| . . . him.| . . . lady.|*; Lucas prints as three lines, dividing . . . *me| . . . him.| . . . lady.|*.

338–9   Q prints as two lines, dividing . . . *there!| . . . remember,|*; Dyce prints as two lines, dividing . . . *picture| . . . remember,|*; Hazlitt and Lucas print as three lines, dividing . . . *there!| . . . picture| . . . remember,|*.

344   Q and Lucas print as two lines, with a new speech-prefix for 344b; Dyce prints as one line; Hazlitt prints as two lines.

358, 361, 368, 372, 381, 382, 389 Q, Dyce, Hazlitt and Lucas print as two lines.

IV. i, 1–2   Q divides . . . *her| Belly* . . .; Dyce divides . . . *that| In* . . .; Hazlitt and Lucas divide . . . *belly,| Will* . . .

10   Q, Dyce, Hazlitt and Lucas print as two lines.

12–13   Q divides . . . *cheese| Wrapped* . . .; Dyce, Hazlitt and Lucas divide . . . *them,| Or* . . .

13, 18, 22, 31, 34, 36, 41 Q, Dyce, Hazlitt and Lucas print as two lines.

42–4   Q, Dyce and Hazlitt print as four lines, dividing . . . *labour.| . . . long,| . . . service.| . . . methinks.|*; Lucas prints as five lines, dividing . . . *labour.| . . . drunk| . . . service.| Sir,| . . . methinks.|*

47–8   Q, Dyce and Hazlitt print as one line; Lucas prints as two lines.

68   Q, Dyce, Hazlitt and Lucas print as two lines.

71   Q, Hazlitt and Lucas print as two lines; Dyce prints as one line.

81–2   Q, Dyce, Hazlitt and Lucas print as three lines, dividing . . . *on't.| . . . honeste'?| . . . sir;|*.

89   Q, Dyce, Hazlitt and Lucas print as two lines.

95–7   Q and Hazlitt print as three lines, dividing . . . *suit.| . . . penitence.| . . . world,|*; Dyce and Lucas print as

five lines, dividing ... *suit.*| ... *fruit*| ... *penitence.*|
... *case*| ... *world,*|.

108–10   Q prints as three lines, dividing ... *Judgement!*| ...
him| ... *be.*|; Dyce prints as four lines, dividing ...
think| ... *Judgement!*| ... *business*| ... *be.*|;
Hazlitt and Lucas print as four lines, dividing ...
think| ... *Judgement!*| ... *him*| ... *be.*|.

IV. ii, 8–9a   Q, Dyce, Hazlitt and Lucas print as three lines.

9b   Q prints as a separate line; Dyce, Hazlitt and Lucas
print as continuous prose with 10 ff.

18–19   Q divides ... *born:*| *As* ...; Dyce, Hazlitt and Lucas
divide ... *with*| *Fore* ...

24–5   Q, Dyce, Hazlitt and Lucas print as four lines.

27   Q and Lucas print as two lines, dividing ... *notes.*|
No ...; Dyce and Hazlitt print as three lines.

30–1   Q and Lucas print as three lines, dividing ... *pre-
sently.*| ... *sir.*| ... *you.*|; Dyce prints as three lines,
dividing ... *yet?*| ... *sir.*| ... *you:*|; Hazlitt prints
as four lines, dividing ... *presently.*| ... *yet?*| ...
sir.| ... *you:*|.

30   Q and Lucas have speech-prefix SAN. between ...
presently.| and *Have* ...

34   Q, Dyce, Hazlitt and Lucas print as two lines.

35–7   Q and Lucas print as four lines, dividing ... *neither,*|
... *them.*| ... *is't?*| ... *you,*|; Dyce prints as five
lines, dividing ... *Spain*| ... *better*| ... *them.*| ...
is't?| ... *you,*|; Hazlitt prints as four lines, dividing
... *Spain*| ... *them.*| ... *is't?*| ... *you,*|.

39, 47   Q, Dyce, Hazlitt and Lucas print as two lines.

49–51   Q prints as prose; Dyce, Hazlitt and Lucas print as
three lines, dividing ... *occasion*| ... *hour*| ...
angry.|.

51–2   aligned in Q.

56   Q, Dyce, Hazlitt and Lucas print as two lines.

60   Q, Dyce and Hazlitt print as two lines; Lucas prints
as three lines, dividing ... *lord,*| ... *accuser?*| ...
mother.|.

64–5   Q and Hazlitt print as three lines, dividing ...
losses.| ... *favour:*| ... *accusation,*|; Dyce and
Lucas print as three lines, dividing ... *losses.*| ...
you| ... *accusation.*|.

77   Q and Hazlitt print as one line; Dyce and Lucas
print as two lines, dividing ... *lord,*| *I* ...

83–4   Q, Hazlitt and Lucas print as three lines, dividing

... *sentence.| ... fear.| ... earthquakes,|*; Dyce
prints as four lines, dividing *... sentence.| ...
confident;| ...fear.| ... earthquakes,|*.

88–9   Q and Hazlitt print as two lines, dividing *...
purpose.| ... entreaty:|*; Dyce and Lucas print as
three lines, dividing *... were| ... purpose.| ...
entreaty:|*.

123, 134 Q, Dyce, Hazlitt and Lucas print as two lines.

137–8   Q and Hazlitt print as three lines, dividing *...
John.| ... side-| ... so?*; Dyce and Lucas print as
four lines, dividing *... John.| ... thee,| ... side-|
... so?|*.

143, 148 Q, Dyce, Hazlitt and Lucas print as two lines.

150–52 Q and Hazlitt print as four lines, dividing *...
bastard.| ... mother,| ... side.| ... accuser.|*; Dyce
and Lucas print as five lines, dividing *... bastard.|
... bastard!| ... hot ... | side.| ... accuser.|*.

153–5   Q prints 153–155a as prose; 153b as a separate line;
Dyce and Lucas print as four lines, dividing *...
married| ... time| ... begetting?| ... business.|*;
Hazlitt prints as three lines, dividing *... married|
... begetting?| ... business.|*.

159–60 Q, Dyce, Hazlitt and Lucas print as four lines.

166–7   Q and Hazlitt print as three lines, dividing *...
mother.| ... tedious.| ... word.|*; Dyce and Lucas
print as four lines, dividing *... mother.| ... proofs,|
... tedious.| ... word.|*.

182–3   Q and Lucas print as two lines; Dyce and Hazlitt
print as one line.

186–8   Q and Hazlitt print as five lines, dividing *... re-
turned.| ... lambskin.| ... thee.| ... of't.| ...
prating.|*; Dyce and Lucas print as six lines, dividing
*... returned.| ... lambskin.| ... thee.| ... buttock|
... of't.| ... prating.|*.

198, 219 Q, Dyce, Hazlitt and Lucas print as one line.

220–2   Q prints 220–222a as continuous prose, with 222b on
a separate line; Dyce, Hazlitt and Lucas print as
four lines of verse, dividing *... else:| ... open| ...
cases.| ... enough;|*.

230   Q, Dyce, Hazlitt and Lucas print as two lines.

254–5   Q divides *... devilishly|How ...*; Dyce, Hazlitt and
Lucas divide *... happed| Gentlewoman ...*

265–6   Q and Lucas divide *... it| Privately ...*; Dyce and
Hazlitt divide *... privately| To ...*

271–2 Q divides ... *daughter.*| *Oh* ...; Dyce, Hazlitt and Lucas divide ... *that's*| *My* ...

272, 278, 292 Q, Dyce, Hazlitt and Lucas print as two lines.

293–6 Q and Hazlitt divide ... *one,*| ... *example,*| ... *mercy*| ... *tempests.*|; Dyce and Lucas divide ... *forsake*| ... *compare*| ... *mercy*| ... *tempests.*|.

299–301 Q prints 299a as a separate line, with 299b–301 as continuous prose; Dyce prints as five lines of verse, dividing ... *bodies.*| ... *seaming lace*| ... *buried,*| ... *tangle.*| ... *I*|; Hazlitt prints as five lines, dividing ... *bodies.*| ... *bones*| ... *buried,*| ... *tangle.*| ... *I*|; Lucas prints as four lines, dividing ... *bodies.*| ... *seaming lace*| ... *buried,*| ... *I*|.

317 Q, Dyce, Hazlitt and Lucas print as two lines.

320–22 Q prints as three lines, dividing ... *in?*| ... *father.*| ... *then.*|; Dyce and Hazlitt print as four lines, dividing ... *in*| ... *Castile.*| ... *father.*| ... *then.*|; Lucas prints as three lines, dividing ... *Castile.*| ... *father.*| ... *then.*|

331–42 Q, Dyce and Hazlitt divide 331–335a ... *begot?*| ... *right.*| ... *touchstone.*| ... *lord.*| ... *seventy-one:*| ... *in't,*|; Q divides 335b–342 ... *pleasure:*| ... *of the*| ... *dealing?*| ... *served*| ... *she?*| ... *waiting-woman?*| ... *baggage!*| ... *tenus.*| ... *gentlewoman?*|; Dyce divides 335b–342 ... *lie*| ... *is there*| ... *mother,*| ... *dealing?*| ... *deposition*| ... *time*| ... *she?*| ... *waiting-woman?*| ... *baggage!*| ... *tenus.*| ... *gentlewoman?*|; Hazlitt divides 335b–342 ... *lie*| ... *there*| ... *mother,*| ... *dealing?*| ... *waiting-woman*| ... *time*| ... *she?*| ... *solicitor*| ... *waiting-woman?*| ... *baggage!*| ... *tenus.*| ... *gentlewoman?*|; Lucas divides 331–42 ... *sure*| ... *right.*| ... *comes*| ... *touchstone.*| ... *lord.*| ... *Lepanto*| ... *time,*| ... *there*| *mother,*| ... *dealing?*| ... *deposition*| ... *time*| ... *she?*| ... *solicitor*| ... *waiting-woman?*| ... *baggage!*| ... *tenus.*| ... *gentlewoman?*|.

343–4 Q and Hazlitt print as verse, dividing ... *dealt*| *In* ...; Dyce and Lucas print as prose.

347 Q, Dyce and Lucas print as prose; Hazlitt prints as verse, dividing ... *said*| *He* ...

348–9 Q, Dyce and Lucas print as prose; Hazlitt prints as verse, dividing ... *viol,*| *For* ...

350–1   Q, Dyce and Lucas print as prose; Hazlitt prints as verse, dividing ... *ever| Know* ...

352   Q prints as two lines of verse, dividing ... *lord| But* ...; Hazlitt prints as two lines of verse, dividing ... *him| To* ...; Dyce and Lucas print as prose.

353–4   Q, Dyce and Hazlitt print as verse, dividing ... *business| And* ...; Lucas prints as prose.

356–7   Q and Lucas print as one line; Dyce and Hazlitt print as two lines.

359–66   Q and Hazlitt print as nine lines of verse, dividing ... *slippers,| ... noise,| ... house.| ... there,| ... slippers?| ... Latin,| ... court| ... counting-house,| ... office.|*; Dyce and Lucas print as prose.

367   Q prints as two lines of verse, dividing ... *one,| To* ...; Dyce and Lucas print as prose; Hazlitt prints as a single line of verse.

368–75   Q and Hazlitt print as eight lines of verse, dividing ... *way,| ... abroad| ... him.| ... business.| ... leave.| her ... appointment| ... refuse,| ... drink.|*; Dyce and Lucas print as prose.

380–1   Q and Hazlitt print as verse, dividing ... *lord:| ... extremely,| ... bed,|*; Dyce and Hazlitt print as prose.

383–5   Q, Dyce and Lucas print as prose; Hazlitt prints as verse, dividing ... *my| ... dealing| ... only| ... better.|*.

388–9   Q, Dyce and Lucas print as prose; Hazlitt prints as verse, dividing ... *please| Your* ...

391, 394   Q, Dyce, Hazlitt and Lucas print as two lines.

395–8   Q and Hazlitt print as verse, dividing ... *elder:| ... plagues,| ... up| ... codpiece.| ... then?|*; Dyce and Lucas print as prose.

403–4   Q and Hazlitt print as two lines, dividing ... *sentence.| ... done:|*; Dyce and Lucas print as three lines, dividing ... *proceed| ... sentence.| ... done:|*.

408–9   Q prints as four lines, dividing ... *husband?| ... that?| ... never.| ... her,|*; Dyce prints as six lines, dividing ... *absence| ... husband?| Never.| ... that?| ... never.| ... her,|*; Hazlitt prints as five lines, dividing ... *husband?| Never.| ... that?| ... never.| ... her,|*; Lucas prints as five lines, dividing ... *absence| ... husband?| ... that?| ... never.| ... her,|*.

416–20   Q prints as seven lines, dividing ... *it.| ... lord.|*

... *face*/ ... *on.*/ ... *lord.*/ ... *gentlewoman,*/ ...
you./; Dyce and Hazlitt print as nine lines dividing
... *time.*/ .... *it.*/ ... *lord.*/ ... *face*/ ... *on.*/ ... *it.*/
... *lord.*/ ... *gentlewoman,*/ ... *you.*/; Lucas prints
as seven lines, dividing ... *it.*/ ... *lord.*/ ... *see't,*/
... *on.*/ ... *lord.*/ ... *gentlewoman,*/ ... *you.*/.

422, 425, 446   Q, Dyce, Hazlitt and Lucas print as two lines.

449   Q, Hazlitt and Lucas print as one line; Dyce prints
           as two lines, dividing ... *Sir,*/ *I* ...

477   Q, Dyce, Hazlitt and Lucas print as two lines.

480–1   Q, Dyce and Hazlitt print as two lines, dividing ...
           tail./ ... *now?*/; Lucas prints as three lines, dividing
           ... *fear,*/ ... *tail.*/ ... *now?*/.

486–7   Q and Hazlitt print as verse, dividing ... *thing,*/
           And ...; Dyce and Lucas print as prose.

489–95   Q and Hazlitt print as eight lines of verse, dividing
           ... *you,*/ ... *twenty:*/ ... *bean-flour,*/ ... *teeth,*/ ...
           farrier/ ... *age.*/ ... *woman,*/ ... *thus.*/; Dyce and
           Lucas print as prose.

511–12   Q and Hazlitt divide ... *impose,*/ *I* ...; Dyce and
           Lucas divide ... *court*/ *Can* ...

514–15   Q and Hazlitt print as two lines, dividing ... *myself.*/
           ... *window*/; Dyce and Lucas print as three lines,
           dividing ... *now*/ ... *myself.*/ ... *window*/.

518–19   Q, Dyce and Hazlitt print as three lines, dividing ...
           indeed!/ ... *longer!*/ ... *Ercole.*/; Lucas prints as
           four lines, dividing ... *indeed!*/ ... *shell*/ ... *longer!*/
           ... *Ercole.*/

523   Q, Dyce, Hazlitt and Lucas print as two lines.

534   Q, Hazlitt and Lucas print as one line; Dyce prints
           as two lines, dividing ... *bed,*/ *And* ...

543   Q, Hazlitt and Lucas print as one line; Dyce prints
           as two lines, dividing ... *thing*/ *I* ...

547–8   Q, Hazlitt and Lucas divide ... *credit:*/ *She* ...;
           Dyce divides ... *she*/ *That* ...

552–4   Q prints as four lines, dividing ... *you*/ ... *accusa-*
           tion?/ ... *Contarino.*/ ... *meeting.*/; Dyce prints as
           five lines, dividing ... *be*/ ... *accusation?*/ ...
           Contarino./ ... *bore*/ ... *meeting.*/; Hazlitt prints
           as four lines, dividing ... *be*/ ... *accusation?*/ ...
           Contarino./ ... *meeting.*/; Lucas prints as four lines,
           dividing ... *forward*/ ... *accusation?*/ ... *Contarino.*/
           ... *meeting.*/.

560   Q, Dyce, Hazlitt and Lucas print as two lines.

568–71 Q prints as five lines, dividing ... *you.| ... sweat| ... Malta.| ... nation| ... father|*; Dyce prints as six lines, dividing ... *you.| ... and I| ... Malta.| ... nation| ... soldiers.| ... father|*; Hazlitt prints as six lines, dividing ... *you.| ... sweat| ... Malta.| ... nation| ... soldiers.| ... father|*; Lucas prints as six lines, dividing ... *you.| ... me,| ... together| At Malta.| ... known| ... father.*

581–3 Q, Hazlitt and Lucas print as four lines, dividing ... *thee,| ... kidneys.| ... murder,| ... there,|*; Dyce prints as four lines, dividing ... *it| ... kidneys.| ... defendant| ... there,|.*

593 Q, Dyce, Hazlitt and Lucas print as two lines.

597–8 Q and Hazlitt print as three lines, dividing ... *wild-fire| ... you.| ... today|*; Dyce and Lucas print as three lines, dividing ... *Ercole's| ... you.| ... today?|.*

607–8 Q and Hazlitt divide ... *strange| Law-suit* ...; Dyce and Lucas divide ... *law-suit| We* ...

V. i, 4–6 Q, Dyce and Hazlitt print as five lines, dividing ... *yet.| ... part.| ... veil| ... face?| ... truth,|*; Lucas prints as six lines, dividing ... *yet.| ... truth| ... part.| ... veil| ... face?| ... truth,|.*

8–9 Q and Hazlitt print as two lines, dividing ... *respected friend.| ... child?|*; Dyce and Lucas print as three lines, dividing ... *respected friend.| Say friend,| ... child?|.*

10 Q and Lucas print as one line; Dyce prints as two lines, dividing ... *sure.| ... first| Of* ...; Hazlitt prints as two lines, dividing ... *sure.| ... know| Of* ...

18–19 Q, Dyce, Hazlitt and Lucas print as four lines.

22, 24, 27, 30 Q, Dyce, Hazlitt and Lucas print as two lines.

33 Q and Lucas print as two lines, dividing ... *Whither?| ... whither.|*; Dyce and Hazlitt print as three lines.

38–9 Q and Hazlitt print as three lines, dividing ... *Roman.| ... then.| ... letter|*; Dyce prints as four lines, dividing ... *Roman.| ... mean| ... then.| ... letter|.*

41 Q, Dyce, Hazlitt and Lucas print as two lines.

V. ii, 1–7 Q, Dyce and Lucas print as prose; Hazlitt prints as verse, dividing ... *you| ... law-flesh!| ... may.| ..*

for't.| . . . backs| . . . fools,| . . . at them.| . . . of them.|
. . . vild| . . . in't.|.

12–13   Q and Hazlitt print as verse, dividing . . . *overtaken|*
And . . .; Dyce and Lucas print as prose.

26   Q, Dyce, Hazlitt and Lucas print as two lines.

31   Q and Lucas print as two lines, dividing . . . *letter?|*
Yes,| . . .; Dyce and Hazlitt print as three lines.

36–7   Q and Hazlitt print as two lines, dividing . . . *villian!|*
. . . issue,|; Dyce and Lucas print as three lines,
dividing . . . *villain!| I protest| . . . issue,|.*

38–40   Q, Dyce, Hazlitt and Lucas print as six lines.

V. iii, 1–2   Q, Dyce, Hazlitt and Lucas print as four lines.

7   Q, Dyce, Hazlitt and Lucas print as two lines.

12–13   Q divides . . . *old| Mistress . . .*; Dyce, Hazlitt and
Lucas divide . . . *mistress,| For . . .*

15   Q, Dyce, Hazlitt and Lucas print as two lines.

17–19   Q prints as four lines, dividing . . . *him.| . . . judge.|*
. . . heard me| . . . believe me.|; Dyce prints as five
lines, dividing . . . *him.| . . . then| . . . judge.| . . .*
tell| . . . believe me.|; Hazlitt prints as four lines,
dividing . . . *him.| . . . judge.| . . . tell| . . . believe*
me.|; Lucas prints as five lines, dividing . . . *him.|*
. . . then| . . . judge.| . . . heard me| . . . believe me.|.

20–1   Q prints as two lines, dividing . . . *Capuchin?| . .*
mistress|; Dyce, Hazlitt and Lucas print as three
lines, dividing . . . *Capuchin?| . . . cannot| . . .*
mistress|.

31   Q, Dyce, Hazlitt and Lucas print as two lines.

V. iv, 1–3   Q and Hazlitt print as prose; Dyce and Lucas print
as three lines of verse, dividing . . . *on't,| . . .*
foolishly:| . . . it?|.

8, 26, 29, 31   Q, Dyce, Hazlitt and Lucas print as two lines.

48–9   Q, Dyce, Hazlitt and Lucas print as four lines.

59–60   Q and Hazlitt print as three lines, dividing . . .
tempered?| . . . practice.| . . . know,|; Dyce and Lucas
print as four lines, dividing . . . *tempered?| . . . know,|*
. . . practice.| . . . know,|.

61   Q, Dyce, Hazlitt and Lucas print as two lines.

63–4   Q and Hazlitt divide . . . *case,|I . . .*; Dyce and
Lucas divide . . . *laugh|At . . .*

64–6   Q and Hazlitt print as four lines, dividing . . .
shadow.| . . . coward?| . . . Christian.| . . . continue|;
Dyce prints as four lines, dividing . . . *you| . . .*
coward?| . . . Christian.| . . . continue|; Lucas prints

as five lines, dividing ... *shadow.| ... coward?| ...
you| ... Christian.| ... continue|*.

72, 76   Q, Dyce, Hazlitt and Lucas print as two lines.

78–9   Q and Hazlitt print as three lines, dividing ... *neck.|
          ... strength.| ... will,|*; Dyce and Lucas print as
          four lines, dividing ... *neck.| ... foil,| ... strength.|
          ... will,|*.

81   Q, Dyce, Hazlitt and Lucas print as two lines.

84–5   Q and Hazlitt print as three lines, dividing ...
          stomach.| ... death?| ... death|; Dyce and Lucas
          print as four lines, dividing ... *stomach.| ... feed,|
          death?| ... death|*.

92   Q, Dyce, Hazlitt and Lucas print as two lines.

151   Q, Hazlitt and Lucas print as two lines; Dyce prints
          as one line.

152   Q, Dyce, Hazlitt and Lucas print as two lines.

166   Q, Hazlitt and Lucas print as one line; Dyce prints
          as two lines, dividing *Ay, ay,|He* ...

177   Q, Dyce, Hazlitt and Lucas print as two lines.

V. v, 3, 10   Q, Dyce, Hazlitt and Lucas print as two lines.

23–4   Q prints as prose; Dyce and Lucas print as verse,
          dividing ... *casement|That* ...; Hazlitt prints as
          verse, dividing ... *that|Looks* ...

V. vi, 4   Q and Lucas print as two lines, dividing ... *Nothing|
          Have* ...; Dyce and Hazlitt print as three lines.

15–16   Q and Hazlitt print as one line; Dyce and Lucas
          print as two lines.

20, 24, 25   Q, Dyce, Hazlitt and Lucas print as two lines.

26–8   Q prints as four lines, dividing ... *life.| ... too.| ...
          Honour| ... abused!|*; Dyce and Lucas print as five
          lines, dividing ... *life.| ... not| ... too.| ... inso-
          lently| ... abused!|*; Hazlitt prints as four lines,
          dividing ... *life.| ... too.| ... insolently| ... abused!|*.

33   Q, Dyce, Hazlitt and Lucas print as two lines.

66–7   Q prints as three lines, dividing ... *you,| ...
          principal.| ... you:|*; Dyce and Hazlitt print as four
          lines, dividing ... *receiving| ... principal.| ...
          lord.| ... you;|*; Lucas prints as three lines, dividing
          ... *receiving| ... principal.| ... you,|*.

75   Q, Dyce, Hazlitt and Lucas print as two lines.

Printed in Great Britain by
The Garden City Press Limited
Letchworth, Hertfordshire SG6 1JS